ACCELERATE TO GLORY

A to Z Keys to Success

Emelia Adjei

Accelerate to Glory

Authored by **Emelia Adjei**

Written and Copyright © 2021

All rights reserved. No part of this publication may be reproduced, distributed or transmitted in any form or by any means, including photocopying, recording, or other electronic or mechanical methods, without the prior written permission of the publisher, except in the case of brief quotations embodied in critical reviews and certain other noncommercial uses permitted by copyright law. For permission requests, write to the publisher, addressed "Attention: Permissions Coordinator," at the address below.

Emelia Adjei/Rejoice Essential Publishing

PO BOX 512

Effingham, SC 29541

www.republishing.org

Unless otherwise indicated, scripture is taken from the King James Version.'

Scriptures taken from the Holy Bible, New International Version®, NIV®. Copyright © 1973, 1978, 1984, 2011 by Biblica, Inc.™ Used by permission of Zondervan. All rights reserved worldwide. www.zondervan.com The "NIV" and "New International Version" are trademarks registered in the United States Patent and Trademark Office by Biblica, Inc.™

Accelerate to Glory/Emelia Adjei

ISBN-13: 978-1-956775-04-4

DEDICATION

The book is dedicated to God and my daughter, Aisha. You're a blessing and a joy in my life. Mum loves you so much, XoXo.

TABLE OF CONTENTS

TESTIMONIALS..vi
ACKNOWLEDGEMENTS..vii
INTRODUCTION...1
ACCELERATE...3
GLORY..3
ACTION...4
ATTITUDE..6
BALANCE...8
BOLD...10
COMMITMENT..12
COMMUNICATION...14
DETERMINATION..16
DREAMS..18
ETIQUETTE...20
EXPLORE..22
FAITH..24
FOCUS...26
GOAL...28
GRATITUDE..30
HARDWORK...32
HONOR...34
INSPIRATION...36
INTEGRITY..38
JOY..40
JUGGLE...42
KINDNESS..44
KNOWLEDGE..46
LEARNING...48
LISTENING..50

MENTOR	52
MINDSET	55
NEGOTIATE	57
NETWORKING	60
OPPORTUNITY	63
ORDER	65
PERSISTENCE	67
PLAN	69
QUEST	71
QUESTION	73
RELATIONSHIP	76
REINVENT	78
SERVE	80
SIMPLICITY	82
TENACITY	84
TIME	86
UNCLUTTER	88
UPLIFT	90
VISION	92
VISUALIZE	94
WIN	96
WISDOM	98
XENIAL	100
XEROPHYTIC	102
YEARN	104
YIELD	106
ZEAL	108
ZEST	119
ABOUT THE AUTHOR	112
REFERENCES	114

TESTIMONIALS

Accelerate To Glory is a great book that anyone who desire to dream again and see it come to pass should get. The step by step principles are such powerful tools to get you back on your feet. It's a reader-friendly. I believe whoever applies the principles in the book will live a spectacular life.

~ Hannah Adjei

This book is a MUST for every home library. If an individual cannot accelerate their growth personally or professionally from reading this book, then I have to declare there is no hope. This book 'rescues' on every.

~ Angel Barrino

A to Z principles concisely brought into light a path to greater happiness and success. I appreciate Adjei's use of both biblical and contemporary quotes to support her message. Accelerate to Glory has helped me become more aware of my power over my own life.

~ Anonymous

Emelia is a committed and organized author, which shows in the setup of the book. Her willingness to ponder over arranging and organizing the principles from A-Z makes it easier for readers to remember and apply to their lives shows her thoughtful personality. The old saying, "Don't judge a book by its cover." applies. Read the book to transform your life and accelerate to glory.

~ Sandra Johnson, Founder of The Lovelight Retreat.

An aura of joy and optimism surrounds author Emelia Adjei. She is a living example of Christian life and love in the modern world. Although challenged by life as a working wife and mother, Emelia finds strength and inspiration in her religion. She applies the principles of Christianity to all aspects of living in a busy American society. This philosophy has been the catalyst of success in Emelia's life.

In the book, Emelia shares simple but powerful practices to improve emotional, professional, and spiritual well-being. Her words are truly motivating and inspirational. Emelia concisely leads readers to an empowering lifestyle that results in the honest fulfillment of personal and professional goals and dreams.

~ Maureen Kane, Educator

ACKNOWLEDGEMENTS

I thank God for giving me the vision and wisdom to write this book. God has been good to me with his grace and mercies.

To the Pastors and mentors in my life, thanks for your prayers and encouragement. Thank you for your words of encouragement which mean a lot to me.

To my few close friends, thanks for being there, showing genuine love and concern through life challenges.

Last but not the least, thank YOU for purchasing and reading the book. Your support motivates me to continue helping and inspiring people to Accelerate to Glory. From the bottom of my heart, I THANK YOU.

INTRODUCTION

Life has a way of strangling us so tight that our dreams, goals, and passion get detoured with no destination. The challenges and trials can make you feel there's no way out. I went through this period for years; I gave up on myself and my dreams, one of which was writing this book. I became frustrated and depressed with myself & life.

I began to have flashbacks; remembering the goals and dreams I had for my life and the thoughts were gratifying. I knew that my calling and purpose were; to inspire and transform lives.

I consciously practiced the principles ("keys") that I have written in this book, quickly noticing dramatic changes in my personal and professional life. I rediscovered myself and started living a purposeful life. Additionally, I used the keys to mentor friends and family and immediately noticed remarkable results in their lives. It would be selfish not to share these keys with the world. It is my passion to teach people how to improve their lives and achieve their goals.

Accelerate to Glory is an exceptional book, a must-read that will change your life, career, and relationships. The keys discussed will propel you to the path of success and fulfillment. The book will also expand your mind, nourish your soul, and refresh your spirit. Even when the tough times come, you will have the tools to stay focused and not give up. It does not matter what you have been through; look to what the future holds. Where you start in life is not as significant as how you finish. You have the power to finish strong and Accelerate to Glory. You've already begun your journey to success by reading the book, share it with friends and family. Thank you and God Bless.

"The person of Jesus prepares you for eternity; the principles of Jesus prepares you for prosperity on earth." ~ Dr. Mike Murdock, Wisdom Center Ministry.

ACCELERATE

- cause faster development, increase the speed or velocity.
- to hasten the occurrence of.
- to progress or develop faster.

"As soon as you hear the sound of marching tops of the poplar trees, move quickly, because that will mean the Lord has gone out in front of you to strike the Philistine army."

~ 2 Samuel 5:24 (KJV)

GLORY

- Something conferring honor or renown.
- State of great gratification.
- A highly praiseworthy asset.
- Majestic beauty and splendor.
- A height of achievement, enjoyment, or prosperity.

"But we all, with unveiled face, beholding as in a mirror the glory of the Lord, are being transformed into the same image from glory to glory, just as by the spirit of the Lord."

~ 2 Corinthians 3:18 (KJV)

ACTION

"All hard work brings a profit, but mere talk leads only to poverty." ~Proverbs 14:23 (NIV)

Action is the process of doing something to achieve an objective. Taking action involves the risk of failing, and most of us freeze in our tracks. Action moves us closer to our goal. It is a by-product of faith. There are obstacles and challenges ahead, yet these should not keep us from moving forward!

"But I'm not ready yet; I need more time, experience, and preparation. I'm still waiting for the right time or a sign." Are these excuses familiar? Be careful not to confuse 'waiting on God' with over-thinking and the fear of failing. Do not confuse seeking wisdom with being overly cautious. Success Coach Lance Wallnau said, "God rewards risk more than caution." Analysis can lead to paralysis.

Action should flow out after a process of inspiration, careful consideration, and preparation. Unfortunately, many get stuck in this process and fail to cross over to the following step-taking action! The difference between success and failure may be a matter of timely action. There is a season and time for everything. Consider nature. The cycles reflect wisdom and order; night and day, death and birth, winter and summer. Planting a garden during fall won't be as fruitful as planting in spring. If you continue delaying your plans, you may miss a window of opportunity.

Action speaks more than words and determines the next set of results. If one's intentions are pure, one will inevitably reap the rewards, but action is first required.

Lance Wallnau said, "You will never feel fully ready because where you are going is always larger than where you have been." What task have you been postponing for ages? Act on it today!

"You must take action now that will move you towards your goals. Develop a sense of urgency in your life." ~Les Brown

ATTITUDE

"Now Daniel so distinguished himself among the administrators and the satraps by his exceptional qualities that the king planned to set him over the whole kingdom." ~Daniel 6:3

Attitude is a settled way of thinking or feeling about someone or something reflected in a person's behavior. If you want to succeed, you must be careful with what dominates your thoughts and emotions.

Contrary to common notions, it is not lack of money or ability that brings failure but the wrong attitude towards life and its challenges. Countless success stories have been born out of the most unfavorable circumstances. Success comes when you face the odds with the right attitude.

Right attitude starts in your head with your thoughts. Having positive and pleasant thoughts keeps you motivated and contributes to good health, happiness, and success. On the contrary, pessimistic thoughts drain your joy and energy; guard your mood to maintain the right attitude. Your ability to respond cheerfully to any task or obstacle with excellence reflects your character.

What is keeping you? Is it a lack of talent, money, connections, or opportunities? Do not turn them to become excuses. Move forward! Change the weather of your life with the right attitude. As corporate sales coach Zig Ziglar said, "Attitude, not aptitude, determines altitude." Success depends on what you do with what you have. Remember to change your mood and environment through a positive attitude!

Have you been entrusted with a responsibility that you don't want? Get a pen and notebook, list five reasons why you should be thankful; then have a cheerful attitude about it and do it!

"The greatest discovery of all time is that a person can change his future by merely changing his attitude."~ Oprah Winfrey

BALANCE

"There is a time for everything, and a season for every activity under the heavens." ~Ecclesiastes 3:1 (NIV)

Balance is mental steadiness or emotional stability when different elements are equal or in correct proportions. Imagine a horizontal balance scale with pebbles on both sides while you stand in the center. The weight is uneven, and your stance is shaky; however, if the scales' weight was made equal, you can stand firm. Lack of balance in our lives does the same. It leaves us in a place of instability. The challenge is to find equilibrium in our daily living. We can accomplish this by prioritizing relationships and responsibilities to achieve a lifestyle that adds value to us physically, socially, and spiritually.

Our existence and growth depend on keeping a balanced lifestyle. Anything in excess is not suitable for our well-being; for example, too much work without rest or fun brings stress down onto the mind and body. We prevent calamity by knowing how or when to practice restraint.

Your activities should reflect a balance of your values, goals, and priorities. The life of an athlete would be strikingly different from the life of a stay-at-home mother due to the responsibilities involved. We must set values and priorities to identify how to occupy our time.

Do you have a balanced life? Three or thirteen years from now, do you think that the things you prioritize today will bear fruit that will make you happy? Our lives must be balanced as our priorities change and grow.

Is there something vital missing in your life? Set a non-negotiable addition to your schedule for resting, vacations, or hobbies. If an activity doesn't fit your priorities, delete it from your schedule, it's a time-waster.

"Just as your car runs more smoothly and requires less energy to go faster and farther when the wheels are in perfect alignment, you perform better when your thoughts, feelings, emotions, goals, and values are in balance." ~Brian Tracy

BOLD

"For this reason I remind you to fan into flame the gift of God, which is in you through the laying on of my hands. For the spirit God gave us does not make us timid, but gives us power, love and self-discipline." ~2 Timothy 1:6-7 (NIV)

Being bold is being beyond the usual limit of conventional thought or action. Bold describes a person showing an ability to take risks or so confident to suggest a lack of shame or modesty. The first kind of boldness is profitable, and the latter is perilous. Either way, boldness is a priceless gift that can shift your perspective radically. Men and women, bold enough to believe in a seemingly impossible dream, have ignited revolutions, whether political, intellectual, or technological.

Boldness exercised in wisdom is courage. Without wisdom, it is foolishness or immodesty! If you are an innately bold person, thank God for the gift, then seek wisdom on using it.

If you are the kind of person who settles for the status quo or does not speak up when your opinion is unpopular, you must be bold and believe in yourself.

True radical innovation or breakthrough only comes through bold people willing to risk, fail, and succeed. You will not always feel confident to pursue new goals, but having the courage to move forward will build your stamina towards your dreams. Humble people can be bold, but they must also be willing to face rejection. One may never know the power they have to inspire others or share their vision. Clarity about purpose brings about boldness as well. Don't hesitate to make a difference. One act of boldness may ripple into a wave that will benefit many generations to come.

Perhaps you are interested in bungee jumping or riding a horse; maybe you need to ask forgiveness from a friend, or perhaps you want to join a singing contest; whatever it is, don't miss a chance to do something courageous in defiance of your fears. Whether you do it for others or yourself, just do it!

"Be bold. Be original. You'll never find YOUR voice trying to fit in somebody else's chorus." ~Lance Wallnau

COMMITMENT

"For if you lay the foundation and are not able to finish it, everyone who sees it will ridicule you, saying, 'this person began to build and wasn't able to finish." ~Luke 14:29-30 (NIV)

Commitment is pledging oneself to a position or diligently pursuing a goal.

It is an unbroken line to a backbone. So it is when every situation, anchored to an unseen aim, keeps everything together. Whatever you engage in, you ought to give your best in terms of time, resources, talent, and money.

Why commitment? Aren't ability, passion, and perseverance enough to bring success?

No matter how accomplished or passionate a person is, if commitment diminishes, then; refocusing one's commitment level is essential for a greater purpose.

Commitment is like sunlight; it shows up every day. Commitment gives consistency and backbone. It is more than just passion because passion dwindles. Commitment requires discipline. Without commitment, life becomes scattered and efforts wasted.

When faced with conflicting commitments in life, seeking wisdom is essential. Decide which path to take and remain committed to the decision. Being committed to a cause has changed history many times. Commitment becomes stronger when directed to a higher cause, to a vision bigger than ourselves. Ultimately, it is a commitment to God and the truth that creates a foundation that strengthens and preserves all other commitments. Is there something you're putting off? Twenty-one days are needed to form a habit. Find someone willing to check on you with the utmost integrity. For the next twenty-one days, stand by your decision to form a new habit or change a bad one. Then, stay committed to the plan with the help of an accountable partner to review your progress.

"If you had started doing anything two weeks ago, by today, you would have been two weeks better at it." ~John Mayer

COMMUNICATION

"A person finds joy in giving an apt reply—and how good is a timely word!" ~Proverbs 15:23 (NIV)

Communication is the impartation or exchange of information or news between two people or a group. The delivery method of the information or message is called the medium or media. Meaningful communication is integral to everyday relationships, successful business partnerships, and excellent work outputs. However, if your communication is flawed, the expected result will also be flawed.

So how can you make your communication effective? Remember these three things:
1) have a clear message;
2) use a suitable medium;
3) have proper feedback mechanisms.

It starts with a crystal clear vision and purpose as to why you need to communicate and what you want to communicate. For example, is your purpose to instruct, remind, encourage, or correct?

Next, choose a suitable medium, whether verbal, non-verbal, to get your message across accurately. Using the wrong medium might communicate the wrong message.

Finally, do not be afraid to request feedback. This last step is a continuous process. Do not just send a message but create a dialogue. LISTEN! LISTEN! LISTEN!

It's vital to open up the channels of communication during difficult situations. If we could be more honest in correcting, more patient in explaining, or more articulate with presentations, we can receive better responses from people. When communicating with another person, remember to be patient, open-minded, and genuine in your intentions and feedback. Diligent efforts are required to perfect the skill and art of communication, understand people and get a message across.

Effective communication is necessary with others when dealing with issues in our personal lives. Most breakups result from a communication breakdown. Do you often find yourself having a "communication problem?" Think of an instance and reflect on how you could have prevented this from happening. What could you have done differently?

"All change, even very large and powerful change, begins when a few people start talking with one another about something they care about." ~Margaret Wheatley

DETERMINATION

"If you falter in a time of trouble, how small is your strength!" ~Proverbs 24:10 (NIV)

Determination is a firmness of purpose—the unshakeable and unstoppable resolve to work until one sees the fruit of one's labor.

Determination is a positive force within you that increases your potential to reach your destiny. It is subtle during times of tranquility, but when circumstances wage war against your dream, the determination becomes ferocious. It grits its teeth and makes its resolve even firmer. How do we nurture our determination to succeed? We begin our journey by stating why we want to pursue a dream or a vision. We must believe in ourselves and our dream no matter what. We must believe that it is possible before taking the first step. Tommy Lasorda, a Major League baseball player with a lengthy career in sports management, said, "The difference between the impossible and the possible lies in a man's determination."

The next step is learning how to handle failure. Realize that failure is not an end in itself but a stepping stone on the path to success. It is a teaching opportunity not to repeat the same mistake or error that caused the problem.

Finally, remind yourself how much you desire to succeed. Determination is a powerful mindset that can influence your actions, especially in times of discouragement. When you are determined, your body does as your mind wills.

President Nelson Mandela of South Africa was imprisoned for twenty-seven years but never gave up since he was determined to fight the injustice of apartheid. There were times when it seemed like he was leading a losing campaign, but his determination kept him from quitting. He knew it was worth it.

Begin to cultivate determination. Nothing is impossible to those who believe. What has you so discouraged that you're ready to give up? Take time to remember three reasons why you should not give up on it. Then list three meaningful moments of success you have had in the past. If you have succeeded in small or big things before, you can succeed again.

"When people are determined, they can overcome everything." ~ Nelson Mandela

DREAMS

"Hope deferred makes the heart sick, but a longing fulfilled is a tree of life." ~Proverbs 13:12 (NIV)

A dream is a cherished aspiration and ambition. Inside each person is a dream waiting to change the world. There are two kinds of dreams, the one you experience when you sleep and the one you imagine when awake.

Your 'sleeping' dreams occur in a fantasy world where there are no limits. Sleeping and aspiration dreams are both called "dreams" for a reason: Your aspirations are usually equally crazy, fantastic, and seemingly impossible, just like your sleeping dreams. So, what do you do with a dream that is 'impossible' when you live in a world of limitations?

Thousands of years ago, a young man had a "sleeping" dream. He liked it so much that he told his brothers about it. In the dream, his brothers were bowing to him. Ha! His brothers hated him for his big dream, his boasting, and his favor in life. Soon, this young man was spending years of his life in a place farthest from his dream being fulfilled—in a national ruler's dungeon imprisoned for a crime he did not commit. He did not know his time in prison was a time of preparation. His fate changed from prisoner to next in line to the king in the blink of an eye!

This man was Joseph, popularly known as 'Joseph the Dreamer.' His story in the Bible teaches us that no matter what, we should keep the dream alive. Learning from Joseph, you should be discreet and humble when sharing your dreams. Beware of dream killers who discourage you.

Instead, connect with people who will encourage and inspire you. Pursue your dream, but prepare to be disappointed many times. Remember, dungeons could just be uncommon pathways towards your dream.

Do you have a "dream board" or a journal where you write your dreams? Make one! It can be a simple notebook or something more creative like a board with photos. Keep the dream burning!

"Hold fast to dreams, for if dreams die Life is a broken-winged bird, that cannot fly." ~Langston Hughes

ETIQUETTE

"Let your conversation be always full of grace, seasoned with salt, so that you may know how to answer everyone."
~Colossians 4:6 (NIV)

Etiquette is a conventional code of ethical and social behavior. It's a proper way of carrying yourself—how to communicate, interact and live with others. Etiquette will help you earn respect, build your image and increase your self-confidence.

Successful people develop not only an expertise in their careers but an overall polish in deportment. They know how to make introductions, dine with dignity, converse on many subjects and treat everyone with respect. They move effortlessly from the conference table to the dining table, paying attention to what's going on, being more aware of non-verbal gestures, and put people around them at ease. In today's fiercely competitive world, etiquette, intelligence, and people skills distinguish one from the crowd and help you outclass the competition. Etiquette also makes forging new and successful relationships much easier.

Proper verbal etiquette is essential, especially in the workplace. When meeting people for the first time, introduce yourself. Always use appropriate titles when addressing superiors or colleagues to avoid undue tension, discomfort, or even offense.

Much of today's interactions are often conducted over the phone or via e-mails; etiquette is vital for effective communication. Proper phone etiquette dictates that you identify yourself with your first and last name when answering the phone or making a call. If it is business-oriented, say your name, your company, and the department you represent. You should also return calls as soon as possible.

Cellular phones are popular, but they can be a nuisance. Try to avoid using them in meetings or when they can potentially cause distraction in public. If you must make or take a call, keep it short and as discrete as possible.

Learn the names of the people where you work. Then, reach out to them regardless of their positions, and acknowledge what they do.

Are you the courteous type who opens the door to women and the elderly and who says "Thank you?" If not, sincerely implement these simple gestures, and see how it makes you and others feel.

"Good manners have much to do with the emotions. To make them ring true, one must feel them, not merely exhibit them." ~Amy Vanderbilt

EXPLORE

"But small is the gate and narrow the road that leads to life, and only a few find it." ~Matthew 7:14 (NIV)

To explore means to find new or different ways to solve a problem, complete a task, or attempt something new. The process requires patience and courage until you accomplish the desired results.

The two worlds in life worthy of exploration are the world around you and the world inside you. There is no discovery without exploration, and there is no exploration where there is no courage to cross boundaries. So, are you eager to explore the unknown, or are you hesitant to step out?

Discovery has a cost, whether it's a new dish, an unknown culture, or an unconquered profession. But, if you have the courage and willingness to try new or difficult things, you can discover your purpose. Exploring the world around you enables you to understand what is inside you—what drives and amazes you.

Exploration is the only answer to life's questions. Have you ever tested your limits and found that you can go beyond what you thought yourself capable? Your spirit is bursting with untapped potential. Do yourself a favor. Put on a good pair of shoes and a dose of courage, and explore life.

To explore your purpose, ask yourself: "What makes me come alive and moves my heart? What do I hate most? What am I good at? Is there anything I can do others can't?" If you don't have the answers, find them. Life is an invitation to keep exploring. In exploring the meaning of life, you will discover that the combination of talents, abilities, and passions that you have is not an accident. At the place where these converge, you will find what sets you apart from the rest of the world. You were made for a purpose that no one else can fulfill. It all begins with an open mind, a willingness to risk and fail, and a hunger to learn and discover.

Do something new this week. Try that foreign cuisine you have been hesitant to check out, book a flight to a city you've never been to, or enroll in a beginner's painting class or go dancing, just do it!

"Twenty years from now, you will be more disappointed by the things that you didn't do than by the ones you did do. So throw off the bowlines. Sail away from the safe harbor. Catch the trade winds in your sails. Explore. Dream. Discover." ~H. Jackson Brown Jr.

FAITH

"Now faith is confidence in what we hope for and assurance about what we do not see." ~Hebrews 11:1 (NIV)

Faith is the act of fixing or settling on a purpose, the strength, courage, or willpower in the quest to achieve a goal. When logic tells you there is no future beyond the bend, when your circumstance tells you things are bound to get worse, when your determination has run dry, when your passion is all but used up, only faith can save you.

Faith is not dependent on what you see or what you have; it is much deeper, more resilient. You will come to a place where you will realize that you don't have everything in you to push you forward. You need something beyond your human ability, and that's having faith in God.

Faith means having complete trust and confidence in someone or something. Faith begins with knowing the 'whom' of your faith. For a Christian, this means knowing that God has a plan to prosper your life. Understanding the loving intentions of an infinite God assures us that our life no longer hangs on what we can do but on God.

Faith could mean trusting humanity's innate goodness and ability to choose what is best. Faith pushes us to seek out something that is beyond our usual dose of motivation and hard work. It allows us to believe for the best even when it does not make sense to do so.

Faith is not lukewarm thoughts about a bright future but a belief of absolute certainty. Faith is especially difficult when everything around us is not going right or as planned. You have to pray and build on your faith with the word of God and inspirational messages. Is there anything in your life that is directly the opposite of what your faith dictates? Without faith, success is just a dream. Faith is the force originating from within you that seeks to bring out the potential to reach one's destiny. Make faith declarations and affirmations; for example, declare "I can do all things through God, or I receive my healing" even if you are still in the process of recovering from sickness. Have faith!

"None of us knows what might happen even the next minute, yet still we go forward. Because we trust because we have faith." ~Paulo Coelho

FOCUS

". . . but the one who stands firm to the end will be saved."~Matthew 24:13

Focus is having a clear visual definition, a central point of attraction, attention, or activity. What you put your focus and energy on will materialize; you create a world through focus. Conversely, you will fail with a broken focus. When we focus on something or someone, it means that our attention, our senses, and our energy is on that one thing or person. Simultaneously, we eliminate other things that can dilute our attention. Anything that competes with our attention is called a distraction.

Have you ever tried focusing a camera lens on a particular subject? Objects in the background will blur as your subject becomes more defined. In life, we also have to learn to blur the unimportant things to capture a clearer image of our chosen destination. In other words, this is the art of focus.

Famous TEDx educational speaker Richard St. John interviewed hundreds of successful people from various fields and learned that one of the top three factors for success is -focus. Domino's Pizza founder Tom Monaghan said that the secret to his success is a "Fanatical focus on doing one thing well." Likewise, Microsoft's Bill Gates said, "If you want to be a great software company, you have to be only a software company." You can't dabble in other things. The more focused we are on one goal, the greater the chances of succeeding. The more scattered our energies, the less we will accomplish. We should learn to streamline our activities to focus on the bigger and more valuable goals we have in life.

Today, we face millions of distractions that take our focus off our work. Yet, concentration is like a steady flowing stream with a level current and momentum.

Staying focus is not an easy skill to develop. The only way to learn is by constant practice. Block time for tasks and meeting deadlines; put up a "do not disturb" sign if necessary. Don't distract yourself with unimportant activities.

"Concentrate all your thoughts on the task at hand. The sun's rays do not burn until brought to a focus." ~Alexander Graham Bell

GOAL

"I press on toward the goal to win the prize for which God has called me heavenward in Christ Jesus." ~Philippians 3:14 (NIV)

Without goals, we are easy prey to distraction. A goal is an aim or desired result envisioned by a person. It can be something as distant as losing thirty pounds in a year or something as simple as washing the laundry before five in the evening. Whatever it is, a process is required.

Do you have goals in life? Can you state them clearly? Or are they more like vague thoughts in your head? The first step is to clarify your goals. Having a goal in your mind only makes it dormant. Keep yourself committed and focused by writing down your goals. Remind yourself daily by developing a visual representation of your goals, such as a collage. Goals keep your energy and efforts directed towards the right things and place.

However, while these steps are better than nothing, they may not be enough. Primarily used for performance reviews, the SMART acronym is a practical goal-setting strategy framework. The purpose of this strategy assists a task-oriented manager or employee with setting goals to clarify what will be required to achieve success and share that clarification with others. The SMART system involves establishing Specific, Measurable, Attainable, Realistic, and Time-bound targets to hit. For example, your goal could be losing ten pounds (specific) in two months (time-bound). With measurable goals, we can easily motivate and energize ourselves to keep moving forward.

It is good to set a big goal or a "stretch goal," but the increments that lead to it should be attainable. If you don't set realistic goals, your motivation will diminish. You will gain confidence and momentum by setting small "bite-sized" tasks leading to your ultimate goal. A goal shouldn't be too hard that you become discouraged. Nor should it be too easy and unrewarding. Feel free to adjust your tasks to contain the right mix of challenge and attainability for your goals

Finally, set an accountability deadline for achieving your goals. Additionally, find an accountability partner. As Henry David Thoreau said, "If you have built castles in the air, your work need not be lost; that is where they should be. Now put the foundations under them."

Set a goal for this week and create a plan that begins today. Is there a paint job at home that needs doing? Do you have a report to submit next week? If it's something that takes more than a week to complete, set a goal to finish fifty percent and make a step-by-step action plan. It's time to take your goals seriously!

"Set your mind on a definite goal and observe how quickly the world stands aside to let you pass." ~Napoleon Hill

GRATITUDE

"... give thanks in all circumstances; for this is God's will for you in Christ Jesus." ~1 Thessalonians 5:18 (NIV)

Gratitude is a feeling of thankfulness or appreciation for a gift, favor, or gesture. The word "gratitude" comes from the Latin word "gratia," which means "pleasing" or "thankful."

Keep a gratitude journal to document what you are thankful for at the end of your day. You will realize that goodness and blessings fill your day. Do you know the easiest way to be BIG? Be In Gratitude. Being grateful has the power to transform your outlook on life.

A great way to stay grateful is by appreciating people, moments, and events in your life. Make a list of why you are thankful, and don't leave yourself out. Even bad experiences teach us life lessons, and we should be grateful for the experience to learn and grow. When you look around, you will find that everyone is absorbed in their own world. You set out to fulfill "your" aspirations, yet the journey to achievement is possible only because of all you have received, all that you are receiving, and all that you will receive. When we are grateful, more blessings come our way.

Here is an exercise to try:

- Sit in a quiet place—express gratitude to each part of your body, from your hair to your toes.

Remember the pleasant and unpleasant incidents of your life and think of one or two reasons to be grateful that these happened.

- Remember each night to write at least five things you are grateful for in the day.

Gratitude softens a heart that has become too stiff and guarded. It also builds the capacity for forgiveness by showing love, empathy, and understanding more than beyond one's judgment. Practicing gratitude is not a denial of life's challenges but an ability to discover treasures from what others will consider useless and disappointing.

Take this thirty-day gratitude challenge. Make a note of something for which you are grateful for thirty days. You will realize you are blessed, and there's so much goodness in life. Don't just "be thankful" in your mind; write it in your journal, send a "thank you" card, gift, or call the person and let them know you are thankful.

"Feeling gratitude and not expressing it is like wrapping a present and not giving it."—William Arthur

HARDWORK

"A sluggard's appetite is never filled, but the desires of the diligent are fully satisfied." ~Proverbs 13:4 (NIV)

Hard work means being diligent in laboring and putting effort into completing a task. A hardworking person is full of energy and commitment. The difference between starting a race and finishing a race is work and diligence. Hard work is what takes you from the foot of the mountain to its peak. We are all endowed with different levels of talent, ability, and capacity. However, we're all born with the ability to work hard towards our dreams.

The Chinese are known for having a high regard for diligence and hard work. Chinese parents are usually very strict and require their children to study in school as much as possible. Therefore, when a child fails to have good grades, a lack of diligence or practice is to blame.

How do we develop the value of hard work? First, it is crucial to realize that hard work has its rewards. Without hard work, we will never discover the joy of enjoying its fruits. Hard work gives us a sense of accomplishment, "No pain, no gain and no guts, no glory."

Hard work gives a sense of ownership and increases our confidence. It validates our strength as we overcome obstacles and realize our potential; regardless of what we were born with, we will only succeed if we work hard. We often blame our lack of success on our lack of ability or bad luck. Truly successful people make it to the top, one hard-earned step up at a time.

Are you tempted to give less than your very best on your job or schoolwork? Do you feel like diluting your efforts on a failing relationship? Remember that nothing pays off better than putting all your heart and energy into something.

Choose an area in your life that needs improvement. How can you work harder on it? Maybe you can spend more time listing prospective clients and calling them. Or perhaps you need to polish your presentations. Whatever it is, choose to go the extra mile.

"I'm a greater believer in luck, and I find the harder I work, the more I have of it." ~ Thomas Jefferson

HONOR

"Pray for us. We are sure that we have a clear conscience and desire to live honorably in every way." ~Hebrews 13:18 (NIV)

Honor is respecting, treating, or showing courtesy to another person, indicating integrity and loyalty. We often set a code of standards on how we see ourselves and others. Therefore, when a person exhibits those traits, we consider him honorable.

These standards or traits have evolved throughout the ages. Nevertheless, some traits transcend time, culture, and religion. For example, we all believe in the supremacy of love and compassion. We all believe in courage; we admire integrity and fairness.

Sometimes, when faced with the dilemma of choosing between two values, but when we can choose to uphold the good of others rather than our own, we discover honor. But, sadly, because of individualism, people decide not to value certain traits to get ahead.

In a society, honor lays down an unwritten code of standards that are beneficial to the community. Conversely, lack of honor brings chaos and injustice.

To live an honorable life means to esteem priceless values over personal agenda, even when it hurts. It also means living what we preach and sticking to the rules of the game even when it hurts.

Lastly, honor is something that a higher authority bestows on us once we've proven ourselves worthy! If we live honorable lives, people will show us respect.

Have you broken "codes of honor?" For example, have you lost your "word of honor" because you broke a promise? Determine to fulfill that promise you made in the past. If it's impossible to complete now, do something to make up for it, but don't make promises you cannot keep. Keeping one's honor untarnished is a challenging but worthwhile goal to pursue.

"The most tragic thing in the world is a man of genius who is not a man of honor." ~ George Bernard Shaw

INSPIRATION

"And let us consider how we may spur one another on toward love and good deeds," ~Hebrews 10:24

Inspiration is the urge or ability to do or feel something, influence, motivate or produce a positive feeling for yourself and others. Inspiration is a mysteriously powerful thing. I will never forget one night when I went to hear an artist perform. I was so moved by the experience. I still remember that night as one of the most meaningful in my life. I realized that inspiration could change the way we think, feel and see the world. Inspiration stirs the dreamer in you. It awakens your imagination and revives your passion. I go to bed in a high inspired state and wake up bursting with energy to take on the day. When I am inspired, I can do more. I burst with ideas!

I thought of how I've missed a lot of good things during the days when I allowed myself to wallow in lethargy and monotony. Since music inspires me, why not purposely listen to music as often as I need to get a dose of inspiration? Getting inspired is not a passive activity. If we know what inspires us, then nothing should stop us from encountering those sources of inspiration.

Do you have a list of people who inspires you? You should have a list of people that you admire. What inspires you? You should note the things, places, or activities that rekindle your spirit and energy. Create an inspiration wall with pictures of things, places, and people.

Inspiration gets you going, fuels hard work, and increases one's abilities and self-esteem. People love working with inspired leaders.

Inspiration intoxicates with the scent of success, stirs up hope in you, and gives you a foretaste of what is possible in your life.

Like goal-setting, finding inspiration has to be intentional since life challenges and tragedies happen with no warning sign. To apply this principle, find a person with an inspiring journey to success or triumph over tragedy. Read their personal story and journey, print it out, and tuck it in your journal or planner. Then, reflect on it and draw inspiration from their attitude towards challenges and trials.

"In life, you need either inspiration or desperation." ~ Tony Robbins

INTEGRITY

"A good name is more desirable than great riches; to be esteemed is better than silver or gold." ~Proverbs 22:1

Integrity comes from the Latin word "integritas," which means wholeness. But when we think of integrity, we usually think of moral uprightness or honesty. Integrity goes beyond speaking the truth, including taking responsibility for how you think, feel, and what one does. It includes the genuine presentation of oneself to others by being sincere and morally coherent.

It takes courage to maintain their integrity in the middle of extreme circumstances. Why is integrity so important that we all strive to have it?

As we increase in wealth and influence, we achieve greater trust. If you want greater responsibility, prove yourself to be a person of integrity. Acting with integrity makes you more effective in all aspects of your life.

Perhaps, you've heard the common saying, "Who you truly are, is what you are when no one is looking." If we pretend to be someone whom we are not, we are deceiving others and ourselves. If we always cover up our weaknesses and lie to people about who we are, we won't be living an authentic life.

Integrity is almost always on top of the list of desired qualities in relationships. We can forgive, but it is difficult to forgive those who misrepresent who they are.

We should strive to possess the kind of integrity that people in positions of influence have. We want to be immovable in our convictions. It all starts somewhere. Wherever you begin, make your goal whole and undivided—knowing what is right, speaking, living, and defending it.

Are you the same person when people are watching that you are when no one is looking? Then, there's no better way to build integrity than to do what you promised to do.

Whoever is careless with the truth in small matters cannot be trusted with important matters. ~Albert Einstein

JOY

". . . the joy of the Lord is your strength." ~Nehemiah 8:10

Joy is having happiness and delight within and around ourselves. Remember to celebrate your life, it's a sacred gift, and you are a blessing to this world! But, don't miss what life is all about. Enjoy life day by day, minute by minute, moment by moment. Joy makes life more beautiful, a sense of pleasure, makes you feel good about yourself and others. Joy helps in making life beautiful by improving our personality and healing our lives.

Everyone is in pursuit of happiness. In haste, we tend to settle for quick fixes or temporary solutions to get momentary bliss. As an article aptly puts it, "Happiness that is based on external circumstances may feel good or pleasant, but it does not nourish and sustain; it is fleeting." Rather than pursuing happiness, we should pursue joy. Joy flows from within us. It is lasting when you know how to cultivate it. So how can you have everlasting joy that does not falter regardless of the day's weather forecast?

Since we have already used the word "cultivate," let us use a garden analogy. If you want to grow joy, plant seeds that produce joy. Feed your mind with positive truths; remember God's promises to you in his word. Recall the encouraging words that people have spoken to you, and speak new encouraging truths to yourself. Water these seeds by affirming them in your life.

Planting seeds of joy is not a one-time act. Continue surrounding yourself with people who bring you joy. Spend time with people who make you laugh and exude positive energy. It is essential to weed your garden. Situations, words, or thoughts may cause weeds of bitterness, ungratefulness, or impurity to grow in our hearts. Pull them out as soon as you can. Do not allow others to steal your joy. Soon, you will find yourself picking the fruits of joy from your garden.

Joy will give you strength when you feel like giving up. It has the power to bring healing and renewed energy. It shifts our eyes from hopelessness and reminds us that there are still reasons to smile and laugh despite trials. Joy is also contagious. It comforts other people around you. Being joyful, even during tough times, is not easy. Remember what Thich Nhat Hanh said, "Sometimes your joy is the source of your smile, but sometimes your smile can be the source of your joy."

Choose to rejoice every day. There will always be something in your life that you can rejoice over. Make an exhaustive list and daily add new things that come to mind. Ponder on how blessed you are. A thankful heart is the best soil for joy to grow.

"Joy is not in things; it is in us." ~ Richard Wagner

JUGGLE

"But to each one of us grace has been given as Christ apportioned it." ~Ephesians 4:7

Juggling is doing multiple tasks simultaneously to get a lot accomplished. Life is a balancing act; we have to juggle responsibilities and activities.

Let's look at the magician's amusing trick of juggling objects. Juggling is a neuromuscular phenomenon. Muscle has memory, and as the body learns to juggle, it memorizes space and timing. Juggling begins with throwing just one object up and down with one hand. Then you progress to two objects with one hand, then three, and so on. Then, you can go to two hands. With proper progression and diligent practice, you'll find yourself juggling more items than you ever thought possible. Juggling expands the mind beyond previous limits.

Let us now apply this to life. One definition of juggle is to "cope with by adroitly balancing." So how do we juggle roles and responsibilities?

First, believe that it's possible to learn a new skill. Second, watch how other people juggle activities in their life. Third, the Bible teaches us to be faithful with the little things. Learn to juggle well what responsibilities you have.

You may say that you are juggling many things already and can't start another project or take on extra work. We can only handle so much at a time. Take the time to evaluate your priorities and commitments.

Finally, juggling life's responsibilities is like juggling different objects. Some are rubber and bounce back when we drop them. Some are made of wood, which may be harder to pick up but will not easily break. Some, however, are made of glass, and when we drop them, it will be next to impossible to put the pieces back. When juggling a busy life, remember that more isn't always better. Take care of the fragile blessings God has given you, which include your family and relationships.

Among the many things you are juggling, is there something you should drop right now? Whatever adjustments you make, remember to take care of things that will bring more meaning to your life.

"Do three things well, not ten things badly." ~David Segrove

KINDNESS

"Those who are kind benefit themselves, but the cruel bring ruin on themselves." ~Proverbs 11:17 (NIV)

Showing kindness means extending something of value to someone with no interest in being repaid or rewarded. It may be a smile, a gesture, or a valuable gift. While kindness seems to come naturally to certain people, it is not always easy for others. Sometimes we feel that the price is too costly. Other times, we don't think the other person deserves to receive something for free. We have no idea how powerful an act of kindness brings to the giver and receiver; the benefits are priceless.

Research has proved that the act of kindness makes your brain produce dopamine, which is associated with positive thinking. The brain has its natural versions, such as endorphins. So when a person does an act of kindness, they feel good on a chemical level thanks to the production of these endogenous opioids.

Mother Teresa said, "Kind words can be short and easy to speak, but their echoes are truly endless." To express a compliment only takes a few seconds, but it could mean giving a person the strength to survive a challenging week or keep him from quitting in life. Kindness requires stepping out of our comfort zone. Whenever we feel hesitant to show kindness, we should remember the many acts of kindness we have received. Showing kindness to everyone can shift the atmosphere wherever we are.

There are times when we move to a higher level of giving. Sometimes, you need to go out of your way and comfort zone to extend kindness. It may mean giving away something precious to bring joy to another. But, always remember what the brilliant Anne Frank wrote in her diary, "No one has ever become poor by giving."

Perhaps the most difficult challenge is to show kindness to people we do not like. The Bible tells us that when we offer goodness to our enemy, it will heap burning coals on his head. It also tells us that God's kindness leads us to repentance. The ability to love the unlovable comes from knowing that we are all recipients of love and forgiveness from God and other people. The stories of Christians that showed kindness to criminals have always inspired me. Of course, this is a dangerous thing to do. But I am amazed at how the hardest heart can melt in the face of kindness. Kindness is disarming.

Do a random act of kindness today. Maybe you can bake some cookies and give them to a family next door, bake a yummy cupcake with an encouraging note or Bible verse to someone in distress. Be creative. And don't be afraid to step out in kindness.

"No act of kindness, no matter how small, is ever wasted."
~Aesop

KNOWLEDGE

"The one who has knowledge uses words with restraint, and whoever has understanding is even-tempered." ~Proverbs 17:27 (NIV)

Knowledge means facts, information, skills, and awareness or familiarity acquired through experience or education. What we learn and understand becomes our resource. Therefore, an investment in knowledge always pays the best interest.

Like the expert, knowledge can promote us to a higher level of influence or responsibility. If you're to hire a physicist, you won't hire someone who constantly failed his physics exams unless he's Albert Einstein!

Knowledge is not the same as talent. Talent may be inborn, but knowledge is acquired. Our knowledge, combined with understanding and the right attitude, increases our market value. It makes us indispensable. Don't you love listening to people who know their topic of conversation? Knowledge gives us credibility and earns people's trust.

Study and experience are the paths of knowledge, but pride and laziness will keep you from it. If you want to become a writer, you have to read materials that exhibit excellent writing techniques and develop your style.

In life, we learn about the principles that govern nature, laws that govern our nation, norms that influence people's behavior, and policies that run an office. The wonderful thing about this century is that limitless knowledge is accessible to almost anyone. So many people have documented the results of their studies and the lessons learned. They urge us not to repeat the same mistakes and build on what they have already accomplished.

Pursue knowledge and understanding, and you will go further in life. Combine passion, talent, and dreams with diligent study and acquisition of knowledge.

When was the last time you read an academic book? If you're already a bookworm, good for you! What other avenues do you think can help increase your knowledge? Attend a free webinar, seminar, or conference. There is a world of knowledge waiting for those who want to learn. Investing in yourself brings security that nobody can take from you, pays dividends for the rest of your life, improves your life and finances, brings peace of mind and confidence.

"An investment in knowledge pays the best interest."
~Benjamin Franklin

LEARNING

". . . let the wise listen and add to their learning, and let the discerning get guidance—" ~Proverbs 1:5 (NIV)

Learning is acquiring knowledge or skills through experience, practice, or study; or by being taught. We all understand its importance, especially when we want to excel in a particular field or endeavor. However, learning is not limited to academics or inside the classroom. The desire to learn is an attitude cultivated at a young age. How does one develop a learning attitude? It is vital to have the confidence to learn and replace the lies we've believed with truths that affirm.

In schools today, students lack interest in academics. There are many reasons for this, but it doesn't mean that the students are not interested in learning. They might just be interested in learning something else or are more receptive to a different manner of teaching. There may be other opportunities for an in-depth analysis of learning hindrances, and these may be discussed separately by those more qualified in the field. But here's a thought, once we believe that we are capable of learning, this will break the boundaries of what is possible and impossible in our lives. Once we discover what we are passionate about, learning becomes fun. Formal education and training are important, as well as school-of-life lessons. If one is interested in learning, the world offers free education and teaches us the most precious lessons.

Learning new things will enhance your knowledge of the world. It also gives you joy in teaching others what you have learned. Learning allows you to communicate and understand broad topics and improve your lifestyle. The Internet has brought the world closer than we ever thought. If you want to be successful, then it is a must to learn.

You can learn from books, newspapers, magazines, movies, TV programs, speeches from great thinkers, etc. Some people teach themselves and are called self-taught. You can also learn from your parents, teachers, mentors, pastors, leaders, and friends.

Lifelong learning provides the opportunity to explore and develop natural abilities fully while also remaining open-minded. The more one discovers about history, current events, politics, cultures of other countries, the more they become open-minded and knowledgeable. Learning increases wisdom, helps to adapt to change, and enables one to view the world from different perspectives. Thus, education will enrich your mind and life, bring meaning and self-fulfillment.

"If you don't learn anything new today, tomorrow will be just like today. This means you don't have a future, just a longer today." ~ Dr. Mike Murdock.

LISTENING

"Everyone should be quick to listen, slow to speak and slow to become angry." ~James 1:19 (NIV)

Listening means to hear or pay close attention to someone or something. Listening is essential for effective communication. Contrary to what many think, everyone can become a good listener. Sometimes we fail to understand people because we don't listen to understand. To be an effective listener, we must set aside our personal opinions, be attentive and open-minded.

When we listen, we should lay down our assumptions, opinions, and intentions. We give ourselves entirely to hearing a person thoroughly, even beyond the words a person speaks. If we assume that we know most of the problem, we may miss an important detail that we do not know yet.

A good listener responds appropriately and asks questions. Your body language shows your interest in the conversation, focused eyes, attentive posture, and responsive gestures like smiling or nodding confirm to the speaker that you are present.

Listening is a key to obtaining knowledge and learning. We listen to people for advice, instruction, and direction. When we listen attentively, we learn and understand more.

Good listening skills are vital to relationships. Whether you're strengthening a relationship, resolving conflict, or saving the world, good listening skills provide a lifeline of learning. Who doesn't want to be surrounded by people who listen well? As Leo Buscaglia said, "Too often we underestimate the power of a touch, a smile, a kind word, a listening ear, an honest compliment, or the smallest act of caring, all of which have the potential to turn a life around."

The better listeners we are, the better friends and workers we become. Try asking a friend how they are doing. Then pay close attention to their response, and a simple answer will provide lots of information. A good listener knows that being attentive to what the speaker doesn't say is as important as listening to what he does say. Look for non-verbal cues such as facial expressions and posture to get a complete sense of what the speaker is telling you.

Listening skills allow one to make sense of and understand what another person is saying. In other words, listening skills will enable you to understand what someone is feeling, thinking, and expressing.

"Friends are those rare people who ask how we are and then wait to hear the answer." ~Ed Cunningham

MENTOR

"For lack of guidance a nation falls, but victory is won through many advisers." ~Proverbs 11:14 (NIV)

A mentor is a person who guides another who wants to pursue the same endeavor where the mentor already has some measure of success.

If you were climbing a treacherous mountain for the first time, wouldn't you want to have someone guide you on the way up? As a guide, a mentor shares his experience so that you won't make the same mistakes he did; he provides counsel. He tugs at you when you are starting to get off track. But, more than this, a mentor is willing to do everything that he can to help you gain the knowledge, wisdom, experience, and even inspiration to become successful.

We need to recognize our mentors when they cross our path. Our parents can be our greatest mentors. We can have a few or many mentors, usually someone we honor and admire for what they do and have achieved in life. Some can be there only for a specific span of your life. Some mentors are lifelong, and others are for a season. Consider what William Arthur Ward said, "The mediocre teacher tells, the good teacher explains, the superior teacher demonstrates, the great teacher inspires." Mentoring needs a commitment from both mentor and student, a dedication to learning and growth.

There is no perfect mentor. A student must be willing to learn despite his mentor's imperfections.

Understanding yourself and your needs will help you identify a suitable mentor. It is essential to have a mentor whose goals and vision align with yours; therefore, be diligent about whom you choose.

Look for people who inspire you and who can offer what you need. Then, once you find a good mentor, commit yourself to learn and submit to their discipline.

I also believe that each one of us is called to mentor, if not now, perhaps in the future. Therefore, it is vital to pass on what we have learned and help make a better world. You don't need to have a big name. All you need is a heart to share what you have learned.

If you don't have a mentor or coach, find one. When life gets tough or challenges arise, you will need mentorship to keep you on track and pursue your goals. Who do you think would be able to help you? Step out and ask that person if they can mentor you, if not for a lifetime, at least for a season.

If you are a potential mentor, you may wonder what is in it for you. Why do you want to be a mentor in the first place? As you facilitate and guide the mentee into goal setting and self-discovery, you will gain personal satisfaction and development in your life.

"Mentorship is learning through the pain of another." ~ Dr. Mike Murdock

MINDSET

"Do not conform to the pattern of this world, but be transformed by the renewing of your mind. Then you will be able to test and approve what God's will is—his good, pleasing and perfect will." ~Romans 12:2 (NIV)

There is nothing more limiting than a fixed frame of mind. Mindset is a fixed mental attitude or disposition that predetermines a person's responses to an interpretation of a situation. Our mindset is based on experience and is either true or false. The opinions can be deeply ingrained in our thinking and be very difficult to erase. However, a positive mindset provides direction in your life.

Those who believe that success is an innate ability believe in a "fixed" theory of intelligence. Others believe that success is due to education and training believe in an "incremental" theory of intelligence. Fixed-mindset individuals dread failure because it is a negative statement on their basic abilities. On the other hand, growth-mindset individuals don't fear failure because that learning comes from failure, and their performance can improve.

Whether simple or profound, mindsets have to do with every belief that influences our actions and reactions. They have the power to make us act in a certain way, even without consciously thinking. If something is not working in your life, it could be due to having the wrong mindset.

Associate with people who are working towards a goal and vision. If we assume we already know the formula for success, we will most likely miss opportunities to transcend or change our mindset. Make it a priority to pull down wrong attitudes by feeding your belief system with truths rather than norms that can change. Truth is the foundation of God's Word. The Bible says, "Nothing is impossible with God." (Luke 1:37) Allow this mindset to take over your life. Develop this belief in your mind— that this is your time, and good things will happen. Stop thinking in terms of limitations and start thinking of possibilities.

Can you identify a wrong mindset that you need to break? Perhaps you've made up your mind that your son will never learn good study habits. This negative mindset is not biblical. Ask God to help you realize the lie behind it. Believe and declare that your son is a diligent student and a lover of learning!

"Once your mindset changes, everything on the outside will change along with it." ~Steve Maraboli, author of Life, the Truth, and Being Free

NEGOTIATE

"If anyone forces you to go one mile, go with them two miles." ~Matthew 5:41 (NIV)

Negotiation skills are not just for business or law enforcement. Negotiation is a dialogue between two or more parties intended to reach an understanding, resolve a point of difference, or gain an advantage. We all encounter situations where another person or group can only meet a need. How can we convince people who are not willing to cooperate with us to see the big picture? The art of negotiation can turn such circumstances into a win-win situation. Tactics are always an essential part of the negotiating process.

Kids at a very young age know how to negotiate with their parents. For example, my seven-year-old daughter sometimes wants to have cookies before dinner. I tell her she can only have a cookie when she eats her dinner. She says, "Just a tiny bit of cookie, and I promise I will eat all my meal." We go back and forth till I allow her to have a bite, and she's happy, then she finishes all her food.

The different styles of negotiation allow for three different situations: Distributive, Integrative, and Negotiator dilemma. First, the Distributive negotiation is when the parties compete for a fixed amount or value. Next, the Integrative is when the parties cooperate to achieve a satisfactory result for both.

Finally, the Negotiator dilemma occurs when a business faces a competing claim at the other party's expense.

An individual who enjoys solving the other party's problems while also preserving personal relationships has an accommodation negotiation style. Accommodators are sensitive to the emotional state, body language, and verbal signals of the other parties. As a result, they can feel taken advantage of when the other party places little emphasis on the relationship.

Avoiders tend to defer and dodge the confrontational aspects of negotiating, specializing in tactics and diplomacy.

Collaborators try to understand the concerns and interests of each party. They can, however, create problems by transforming simple into complex situations.

Competitive negotiators are interested in winning but can dominate to the point of neglecting the importance of relationships.

Compromisers can unnecessarily rush the negotiation process and make concessions too quickly but are useful when there is limited time to complete the deal.

Which type of negotiator are you, and what is your weakness as a negotiator? Styles can change over time. Identify your strength and weakness as a negotiator.

Regardless of what negotiation style you have, always remember, the main goal is to create a win-win situation for everyone.

"You cannot negotiate with people who say what's mine is mine and what's yours is negotiable." ~John F. Kennedy

NETWORKING

"Two are better than one, because they have a good return for their labor...." ~Ecclesiastes 4:9

Networking is the act of connecting and exchanging information with people who can help you with an objective or goal for professional or social purposes. A key aspect of networking involves cultivating relationships that will help you advance your career.

However, networking can go beyond career goals. To network is to recognize the value of people in our lives. The quality of a person's social connections depends upon the network he creates. Having a network of friends, relatives, and neighbors is essential for a person's well-being and happiness. In addition, a parent and child bond is an important network to teach social and emotional intelligence for forming strong relationships.

So how does one network? First, make the most out of every social opportunity. You don't need to be an extrovert or compete with others to do this. You just have to go beyond your comfort zone.

After making new friends or exchanging business cards, the next step is finding ways to keep in touch. The easiest way is through social media: Twitter, Facebook, LinkedIn, or other mediums. Always try to stay in touch via email, text, or phone to have a brief conversation.

The key is seeing value in each person, not judging by their status or appearance, and be willing to extend a helping hand. Of course, there will be times when you have to say "no," but even in saying no, simple gestures of communication will say a lot about how you value people.

A simple way to get connected and widen your network is being personable. Smiling implies warmth, welcoming, and caring. Service with a smile is a buzzword of the service industry. Smile has its benefits from personal to social levels. There are no side effects from smiling, and it does not cost a dime. Smiling attracts good energy and brings happiness which is the ultimate goal of all humanity.

As we pursue our dreams and goals, we should reach out and help others in their process, and we need each other to succeed. We need to connect with people we're meant to walk this life journey with as we pursue our dreams.

Have you made any new friends recently? Strengthen ties and send a message via SMS or Facebook. Reconnect with old friends. How about joining a networking event or attending a friend's party to establish new professional contacts? Keep a friendly and people-oriented vibe, and it will be easy to expand your network.

"The way of the world is meeting people through other people." ~ Robert Kerrigan

OPPORTUNITY

"Preach the word; be prepared in season and out of season;" ~2 Timothy 4:2 (NIV)

An opportunity is a combination of circumstances favorable for the purpose or fits the time. Opportunities provide occasions to advance. As the saying goes, "Opportunity knocks but once." so grab it before it lapses!

Some opportunities are not obvious; they show up disguised as a challenge or problem to test your tenacity and passion. As Winston Churchill said, "The pessimist sees the difficulty in every opportunity; the optimist sees the opportunity in every difficulty."

Opportunists are optimists by nature. They can convert threats into opportunities. An excellent illustration for this is a scene from the movie Facing the Giants in which the Eagles, an underdog football team, practiced fighting an unbeatable opponent. The most vital member of the team, Brock Kelley, did not believe they had a chance to win, and his pessimistic attitude was influencing the rest of the team. Seeing how dangerous Brock's attitude was, their coach called him to do the "death crawl." He crawled an almost impossible 100 yards with a 160 pound player on his back, after which Brock realized he had underestimated his physical and mental ability as a player. The coach advised him that his influence on the team is so crucial that Brock can't afford to doubt their team. Brock had a change of heart. In the end, he chose to influence the team positively.

Brock was a threat at first because he did not use his influence to help the team. However, by influencing Brock to think and act differently, their coach turned the threat into an opportunity to encourage the team with Brock's positive attitude.

Pay close attention to the opportunities showing up in your life. Are these opportunities on a golden platter or dressed in work clothes? Are they disguised as threats? Identify one opportunity that is open to you right now. It can be a challenging project or simply an opportunity to stretch your patience in dealing with a stubborn employee. Take the challenge and roll up your sleeves, don't pass up on a chance since you might not have that chance again.

"We often miss opportunity because it's dressed in overalls and looks like work." ~Thomas A. Edison

ORDER

"But everything should be done in a fitting and orderly way." ~1 Corinthians 14:40 (NIV)

Order is a state in which everything is in its correct or appropriate place. According to a particular sequence, pattern, or method, it is the arrangement or disposition of people or things concerning each other. Applying this to our day-to-day life, to practice order means to put things in their proper place in such a way that brings peace and efficiency.

You need to maintain order at both mental and physical levels. A mental order means awareness of your thoughts and the things that you choose to consider. Many people allow their minds to wander throughout the day. That is why people often say this day has passed by so quickly, or "Where did the time go?" The goal is to enjoy each day as if it were the last. But our thoughts must be in the present moment for us to reach this goal.

How does working inside a chaotic room make you feel? What about one that is orderly? The ability to think clearly, organize your thoughts, or handle a chaotic workplace will serve you immensely.

Order speeds up work processes to meet deadlines. For example, let's say I want you to read a paragraph of shuffled sentences. The first sentence is in the middle. The last sentence is first. The second sentence is last, and so on. How long will it take you to understand the paragraph?

Imagine an orderly room with everything in place; furniture arranged properly, smaller items in proper containers, fixtures in their right place; the thought brings a sense of calmness and relaxation. Order turns our effort into quality because we've maximized the space by thinking ahead.

When you know that things in your life are in the right place, whether it's a pair of socks or your schedule for spending time with family, you feel you are in control. If you know which things in your life go together and which things don't, you understand order.

Start bringing order into your life. Take 15 minutes a day, and bring some orders to your workspace, computer, file drawer. Keep this evaluation going in home and personal life.

"Chaos is merely order waiting to be deciphered." ~José Saramago, "The Double"

PERSISTENCE

"Ask, and it will be given to you; seek and you will find; knock and the door will be opened to you. For everyone who asks receives; the one who seeks finds; and to the one who knocks, the door will be opened." ~Luke 11:9-10 (NIV)

Persistence is the firm or obstinate continuing course of action despite difficulty or opposition and not giving up. When you start pursuing your dreams, you have high hopes, fresh confidence, and unscathed knees. However, on your journey, you will pass through briers and thorns. You get cuts and scrapes from slips and falls. During this journey, you experience exhaustion and disappointment. Welcome to the challenge of persistence!

Let's visualize a group of people digging a tunnel with their bare hands. They are digging through rocks, gravel, and dirt. They believe that behind that wall of hard earth is an opening that leads to the light, which represents their common goal. They are very close to hitting the end but feel like giving up. They're tired, bruised, and frustrated, but they continue to dig until the light breaks through.

While pursuing your dreams, you will wonder if it's worth the hassle? You count your failures, your scars, and your numerous disappointments and wonder, will I ever make it?. You make excuses to quit rather than move forward. What if you are only inches away from the end of that tunnel? The road to success is not easy; it's hard, that's why only those who persist succeed.

If we focus on why we should push forward and list the rewards, we will realize the obstacles are just temporal. Setbacks build muscles of determination and faith. I love what Tom Hiddleston said, "You never know what's around the corner. It could be everything. Or it could be nothing. So you keep putting one foot in front of the other, and then one day you look back, and you've climbed a mountain."

The dream journey tests improves, and builds our character. Prove your persistence by taking that next step forward. For example, are you following up on a business transaction? Don't give up after receiving a "no." Instead, ask yourself what you could do to receive a "Yes." Then go and dig some more until that door finally opens. Now is the time to persist.

"We are made to persist, that's how we find out who we are." ~Tobias Wolff

PLAN

"Suppose one of you wants to build a tower. Won't you first sit down and estimate the cost to see if you have enough money to complete it?" ~Luke 14:28 (NIV)

To plan commonly means to devise a scheme, structure, or method to accomplish a purpose. People fail because they "failed to plan" but not planned to fail. You need to plan on where you want to be and what you want to accomplish in life.

Why do we need to plan? Let's use a business start-up as an illustration. Creating a business plan is essential for starting a business. Planning will lessen the risks of failure. For example, imagine we are starting a lemonade stand; if we check the lemon's price but they're too expensive because of the season. Then it is not reasonable to open a lemonade stand out of season.

On the other hand, if we expect a crowd on opening day because of a nearby event. Then we proceed to prepare lemonade for an anticipated increase in sales. Planning helps us make the most of our time and resources!

A plan prepares us for action by helping us avoid mistakes and time wasters. Goals can be short-term or long-term. They can apply to daily tasks, a yearlong strategy, or something that will take years to complete.

No matter how much we plan, we should always remain open to deviations to our plans. Life is unpredictable, though our plans may be many; they are God's plans. The key is seeing value in each person, not judge people by their status or appearance, and be willing to extend a helping hand prevails. Therefore, it makes perfect sense to commit our plans to the Lord and ask Him for guidance before anything else. Along the way, we should be willing to deviate from our plan. Remember, the goal is not the plan itself but the purpose for which we devised a plan.

Do you have a clear and specific plan for reaching your goal? Do you have a habit of committing your dreams to God? Why not say a silent prayer right now? Ask for wisdom on how to pursue your goal for this week. Pray for an effective action plan and write it down. For example, if you want to finish cleaning your stock room, plan to assign 15 minutes a day to work on it, and then set aside half of Saturday to complete whatever is left. Even if you can't stick to your plan 100%, you will make significant progress.

"Plan specifically so you can implement flexibly." ~Dallin H. Oaks

QUEST

> *"But remember the Lord your God, for it is he who gives you the ability to produce wealth, and so confirms his covenant, which he swore to your ancestors, as it is today."*
> *~Deuteronomy 8:18 (NIV)*

Quest is about seeking something meaningful. It's a powerful process for thinking about your ideal future and motivating yourself to turn your vision into a reality. It helps you choose where you want to go in life. By knowing what you want to achieve, you know where you have to concentrate your efforts. You'll also quickly spot the distractions that can, so easily, lead you astray.

By setting clearly defined goals, you can measure and take pride in the achievement of those goals. Setting lifetime goals gives you the overall perspective that shapes all other aspects of your decision-making. It provides balanced coverage of all the critical areas in your life; while providing long-term vision and short-term motivation, raising your self-confidence as you recognize your ability and competence in achieving your goals. It focuses on your knowledge acquisition and helps you organize and make the best out of your time and resources.

Lance Wallnau, business consultant and success speaker, teaches that if we combine our abilities, passions, and values, the synergy of these three can address a need in society.

Everyone has a unique role in society to pursue the convergence of his talents, passions, and values. That role is profitable because only he can fulfill that.

Quest is second nature to the business-minded person since it requires constant research to find solutions. You can develop the skill by learning from business-minded friends how we profit from our talents and gifts. Profit may not necessarily mean money, but it can mean knowing the worth and value of what you have. Some of us may need connections to gain the recognition we need for our art or inventions. Every person has something that another person needs. Think of something you can offer to other people. If you're good at baking, create something. Do you have useful information to share with the world? Start a blog and earn through advertisements. Share something you have that others are willing to give something for in exchange.

"Art is making something out of nothing and selling it."
~Frank Zappa

QUESTION

"For lack of guidance a nation falls, but victory is won through many advisers." ~Proverbs 11:14 (NIV)

Question means seeking to learn, asking, and inquiring to either increase knowledge or clarify doubts. It forms the basis of a problem requiring a solution. It also reveals your passion for learning, growing, and knowing your difference from others. Therefore, you should ask yourself questions daily and give honest answers.

Asking the right questions at the right time is essential for zeroing in on an exact problem; don't hesitate to ask questions when you do not understand. When networking, you need to ask appropriate questions without being judgmental or derogatory. Questions reveal interest and disinterest; ask carefully and wisely.

Asking the right questions will not only save time it will also improve accuracy and success rate. In addition, asking the right questions is an excellent way to gain rapport with others.

Why should we ask questions? One apparent reason is that we don't have all the answers. At times, one can be ashamed or embarrassed to ask a teacher, classmate, or employer when unclear about something. We end up doing the wrong thing.

Asking a question is a sign of humility and willingness to learn. You should not allow pride to get in the way of excellence and success.

Some questions arise from a deep desire to get more out of life, such as knowing one's purpose or calling on this earth. These questions can be rhetorical, revolutionary, or introspective and, if answered honestly, make us free and peaceful.

Other curious questions have led to discoveries in technology and health. These questions can change history or trends in technology. Maybe you've heard of Edison, Bell, or the Wright Brothers? If not for these inventors asking questions, there would be no light-bulbs, telephones, or airplanes.

We all need to reveal mysteries. So do not brush aside questions that nag our thoughts, for they may lead us to discover things that could change our world.

Whether asking other people or whether we ask ourselves, we must learn the patience involved in the process of discovery. And if we are truly hungry for the truth, for a solution, or a great discovery, we should keep asking until our hearts are satisfied with answers.

Is there a question that you have been trying to avoid? Grab your journal and write down three questions that you want to answer. Which of these can you start answering? Some questions we already have the power to answer. Other questions may take time and prayer for answers.

"If you have never changed your mind about some fundamental tenet of your belief, if you have never questioned the basics, and if you have no wish to do so, then you are likely ignorant." ~Vera Nazarian

RELATIONSHIP

"Therefore encourage one another and build one another up, just as you are doing." ~1 Thessalonians 5:11 (NIV)

Relationship is the connection, attachment, association between two or more people. Humans are social beings and do not live well in isolation. It is not difficult to convince people that relationships are indispensable, and many agree that relationships require work. But very few will work hard to nurture and maintain a relationship. Intimate relationships require time, love, and sacrifice to keep them healthy and growing.

Having a romantic or platonic relationship varies from person to person. Relationship fills the emptiness in our lives and provides a sense of belonging. The cornerstones of a good relationship are trust, love, and respect. If you find certain behaviors that cause you not to trust your partner, talk with your partner about this.

Compassion is a key to maintain a relationship; cultivate compassion for a better relationship. Instead of over judging your partner, compliment them. This compassion will create a bond for a stronger longer lasting relationship.

A relationship will go through ups and downs, similarities and differences. It is necessary to have the willingness to forgive as forgiveness brings healing. Forgiveness is perhaps the most demanding part of a healthy relationship.

But no matter how deep the hurt, it will always be worth the effort to reconcile. Nothing can compare to the strength and depth of a relationship that has withstood various trials.

Healthy, meaningful relationships are rewarding, bring gratification, comfort, and protection. Surround yourself with people who are goal-oriented and achievement-driven. You will need the support and encourage you to pursue your dreams. Some friends you know need to become the friends you knew, therefore regularly re-evaluate your friendships.

How do you value the relationships that you have? Which relationship would you like to make better? How can you help strengthen or mend it? Take that one step boldly today. Whether it's by sending a friend a note or by bringing your daughter out on a movie date, take the step. It doesn't have to be anything extravagant; it just has to be a firm step towards making the relationship grow.

"The quality of your life is the quality of your relationships." ~ "Anthony Robbins

REINVENT

"Do not conform to the pattern of this world, but be transformed by the renewing of your mind. Then you will be able to test and approve what God's will is—his good, pleasing and perfect will." ~Romans 12:2

To reinvent is to change something so much that it appears to be entirely new. In other words, it means making significant changes or improvements in a different way. A perfect example is Apple's reinvention of the mobile phone. Before the iPhone, voice calls and text messages limited mobile phones. The iPhone reinvented mobile technology, and we now have the functions of a music player, video recorder, and Internet mobile communicator all in a single device.

Why do we need to reinvent ourselves? So we remain competitive in the marketplace by learning new skills, new marketplace practices, a new language, or adapting to the latest technological trends.

When we encounter significant changes in our lives or our environment, we need to reinvent. It is not changing for the sake of change but evolving in response to life's transitions or challenges.

One example is reinventing one's lifestyle in response to poor health or sickness. For example, are you feeling sluggish due to stress and lack of exercise? Are you gaining too much weight because of too much sugar, cholesterol, and junk in your diet? Maybe it's time to reinvent your lifestyle to give more attention to your mental and physical health!

Reinvention is also a great way to cope in a new environment. Are you migrating to a different country? You'll have to change most of the way you attend to daily chores. Some of the ingredients you cook with might not be available. Why not reinvent your cooking?

Reinvention embraces empowering change. So, don't get stuck doing the same thing repeatedly, especially when there's a better way of doing it.

"Don't make excuses; make improvements." ~ Tyra Banks

SERVE

"Serve wholeheartedly, as if you were serving the Lord, not people," ~Ephesians 6:7 (NIV)

Serve is the action of helping or doing work for someone. Service is an act of generosity. It flows from a desire to help, assist or make a difference in people's lives. Having an attitude of service means looking for ways to help rather than waiting to be asked. The point is to make a sincere contribution giving your best regardless of the assignment. People willing to serve can change the world through their giving.

What does service look like? Service is going out of your way to meet a need. One example might be picking up trash in the park. Another example could be helping an elderly neighbor clear snow from their driveway. How does one develop this virtue? For some, service comes naturally. But others must cultivate the skill by finding ways to help.

The first step towards an attitude of service is to develop sensitivity to another's needs. Some needs are obvious, while others are subtle. To recognize a person's need(s), we must be observant and sensitive, realizing there will be hundreds of opportunities to serve.

Secondly, we must step out of our comfort zones and help by volunteering. To serve someone, one has to overcome the natural impulse to avoid risk or rejection. Serving also means investing your time or energy.

Last but not least, we must serve without expecting anything in return. There will be those that appreciate our efforts and give thanks. However, there will be others that may criticize or condemn. Through it all, be sincere. If you intend to seek recognition, you are bound to be offended when people don't show appreciation.

Service is a gesture of humility that has another person's well-being as the goal. Think of a way you can serve someone today. Go out of your way to add a ray of sunshine to a friend's day. Does your spouse always cook breakfast and do the dishes? Maybe you can volunteer to do it for an entire week. Or do you always ask your secretary to buy you coffee in the morning? Why not take a day or a few days and buy coffee for your entire staff instead? Think of something simple but practical. And don't show off. Just be happy to serve.

"Everyone has the power for greatness—not for fame but greatness because greatness is determined by service." ~ Oprah Winfrey

SIMPLICITY

"But godliness with contentment is great gain." ~1 Timothy 6:6 (NIV)

Simplicity is powerful. We see this everywhere—in art, in technology, and business. According to John Maeda, simplicity in design is "about subtracting the obvious and adding the meaningful." The elements of a design should convey depth rather than state the obvious. Too many unnecessary details competing for your attention result in clutter. Simplicity focuses the eye on what is beautiful. You can apply this to any aspect of life.

Are there things in your life that do not add up to self-improvement? We may miss the beauty of life if we are distracted by so many non-essentials.

For example, if my smartphone has several applications, it could make my phone function slower. On the other hand, if I delete the ones that are not necessary, my phone just might run faster and more efficiently. Are there any "applications" in your life that you can set aside? To achieve simplicity is to acquire power, which begins with knowing what you value most in life. Sometimes, before we can pinpoint which things should remain and which ones should go, we experience a season of clutter, confusion, and lack of direction. But as we sift through the mess, we will find a renewed focus to simplify our life.

Here's how you do it: Remember that which is truly valuable and focus on the basics. Live reflectively and mindfully. Re-assess your definition of what's important. Some things we consider essential today will have no meaning or value a year from now. Should we radically change our perception to have a simple life again?

When we return to God's Word and His purpose for our lives, we find simplicity. It redirects our attention to what is essential, like family, beauty, and service.

Try abstaining, for one week, from something that takes your time and attention. For example, try not to watch television or go online unless work or school requires you to. These are things that almost feel necessary, but we realize that we do better without them the moment we lay them aside.

The better you become at simplifying your life, the better you'll be able to experience what you are doing at the moment and take what it offers you without being distracted by worries about what happened earlier or what might happen next.

"There is a certain majesty in simplicity which is far above all the quaintness of wit." ~Alexander Pope

TENACITY

"Wait for the Lord; be strong and take heart and wait for the Lord." ~Psalm 27:14 (NIV)

Tenacity is the ability to hold on to, not give up on, or prevent oneself from being separated from an object, position, or resolve one has made. It is the state of holding on to an idea or a thing very strongly. It is the quality displayed by someone who just won't quit but keeps trying until they reach their goal. Anything worth doing takes persistence, perseverance, and stubborn determination.

Have you ever played tug of war with a dog? If you are battling over your favorite shirt, the last thing you want is a tenacious dog permanently latched onto it. But this is the emotion and resolve that tenacity requires; gritting your teeth and pouring out your strength to keep something from slipping away.

Could you remember any instance in your life where you exhibited this trait? Tenacity is different from stubbornness. Stubbornness can mean refusal to change, while tenacity is a willingness to adjust to hold on to your goal. It has an element of resilience that withstands storms.

I will never forget a movie about a young man who joined a dog-sled race to save his family's farm. It was a dangerous race that took cold days, snowy nights, and many a battle with sickness, injury, and dishonest opponents. You see this young man named Will, bleeding from the harsh weather and rough race towards the finish line. He had every reason—logical and acceptable to quit! But he didn't. He wins the race at the risk of losing his life. At the end of the movie, the people in the theater rose and roared in applause. As a Danish saying goes, "The next mile is the only one a person has to make."

Tenacity is about figuring out where you are and where you want to be and then making the first step to getting there. Don't spend too much time figuring out how to get there. Yes, you need to know how to get there; you need a map, a business plan, a training plan, a saving plan, and other plans. But don't get bogged down in the paralysis of planning. So what if you take a step in the wrong direction? You get to learn which direction is wrong, and this is valuable! It helps you find out what is the right direction, and you learn more than one good lesson at a time.

Do you need to let go of a dream? Do you have a target that is slowly slipping away? Maybe it's time to tighten your grip and prepare for a wild tug-of-war for your goal. Are you struggling financially? Don't give up on yourself; it's time to relearn how to manage your finances. Go back to the Bible basics of tithing and proper stewardship. The more trials come, the stronger you should hold on to faith and hope.

"When you reach the end of your rope, tie a knot and hang on." ~Abraham Lincoln

TIME

"For he says, in the time of my favor I heard you, and in the day of salvation I helped you." I tell you, now is the time of God's favor, now is the day of salvation." ~2 Corinthians 6:2

Time is the duration in which all things happen or a precise instant that something happens. Have you ever found yourself wishing for thirty-hour days? Most people do so more often than not. But, unfortunately, there's never enough time in a day. The truth is, even a thirty-hour day would not be enough to do everything that needs your attention. Our lives would still have unfinished tasks, unanswered letters, unvisited friends, and unread books.

A simple fact in life is that there is a time for everything under the sun, meaning a precise time or season for everything. Meaning that there is not only enough time for every vital undertaking, but there is also the right and strategic time for each. As the writer of Ecclesiastes said, the result is desirable and beautiful when accomplished at the right time. Therefore, our goal should be to seek wisdom on spending our time to reap the fruits of an intelligently spent life.

We live in constant tension between the urgent and the important. The challenge is how to sort the things we have to do in order of priority. Here's a technique that is no secret to many successful managers. To manage time effectively, one must take time off for planning and evaluation. A prominent businessman once said that one minute spent in planning saves four spent in execution.

There is a true story about a factory manager who asked a successful person for help on how to make his factory workers more efficient. The advice given was for the workers to list the things they have to do according to priority and then follow the list every day. Amazingly, the workers significantly increased their productivity just by following that simple advice!

Aside from budgeting our time, we must also learn to strategize. To value time also means to value opportunities. Is it time to plant or to harvest? Is it time to rest or to work? As we plan our days, we also learn to respond to life's weather changes wisely.

What are the unimportant habits you tend to prioritize over essential but non-urgent tasks? Be honest! Write them down and make a vow to never fall into this trap again. You will save more time for quality rest. It will also save time for you to attend to unexpected emergencies. Do you default to 'Facebooking' when bored? Do you watch television all night long? Instead of spending much time on unimportant things, set a limited time for breaks and accomplish more.

"Yesterday is gone. Tomorrow has not yet come. We have only today. Let us begin." ~Mother Teresa

UNCLUTTER

"First clean the inside of the cup and dish, and then the outside also will be clean." ~Matthew 23:26b (NIV)

To unclutter is to clear, change, modify, make neat and orderly. But, unfortunately, clutter increases stress and a feeling of uneasiness which drains your energy.

A simple way to unclutter your life is by spending 15 or 30 minutes each night to sort out things lying around or piled up. Then, use the weekend for any major clean-up jobs. Either way, you'll remove a subtle but significant energy drain from your life and replace it with feelings of relaxation that come from a clutter-free space.

What does un-cluttering your time, house, and life mean? It simply means throwing away the things that suck your energy or focus. Not every invite or event has to be honored if it doesn't fulfill our purpose. Entertainment is useful for relaxation, but if it has become a compulsion and distraction that drains our energy and efficiency, it's time to cut down.

Let's turn to other kinds of clutter. Many stressed people live in cluttered homes. House clutter is both a cause and effect of a cluttered itinerary. The energy customarily reserved to clean up was used on other things. The clutter in your house adds to your stress because you cannot find peace.

A nightly clearing that takes 15 to 30 minutes is manageable. Just tackle one pile at a time, un-cluttering your house portion by portion. In addition to de-cluttering your house, un-clutter your life from toxic and unhealthy relationships. Take an honest look at your relationships. Which ones are worth maintaining? Which ones would be left alone? Get rid of the over-critical, unpredictable, jealous, and competitive friend or family member. Spend less time in the company of negative people. You will find new space to making new connections to advance your dreams and goals.

Evaluate the things that consume your time and energy. Are you trying to master several unrelated skills all at the same time? Stick to learning animation if that's your passion, and set aside other hobbies like gaming and blogging. Perhaps you can pick up one of those again in the future, but right now, if they're not helping you be 100 percent on something, they are clutter.

"Three rules of work: out of clutter find simplicity, from discord find harmony, in the middle of difficulty lies opportunity." ~Albert Einstein

UPLIFT

"May the God of hope fill you with all joy and peace as you trust in him, so that you may overflow with hope by the power of the Holy Spirit." ~Romans 15:13 (NIV)

To uplift is to elevate or stimulate morally or spiritually. At some point in life, you will have to uplift yourself or have someone help you in the process. It is the act of raising or influencing someone in a positive way to elevate their spirit. It is essential to cheer, support and encourage others of their dreams and goals. Uplift your heart with a message that touches you just when you need it most. All positive thoughts work as a catalyst in uplifting your mind and heart. Uplifting leads to growth, elevating your skills, thoughts, knowledge about life continuously.

We all need encouragement from work stress, disappointment, discouragement, and losing a loved one. Go out and enjoy nature or take a walk. You can change your mood and feelings by changing your environment; schedule some time to relax; enjoy your hobbies, sign up for a class to learn something new.

Watch movies that inspire and uplift you. Surround yourself with people who motivate and inspire you. It makes sense that the habits, attitudes, and behaviors of the people you spend the most time with can rub off on you, so hang out with good people whom you respect and admire to uplift yourself. In addition, reading the Bible and inspirational books will improve your mood.

As a writer, sending letters or a note of encouragement to a friend makes me happy and uplifts my spirit. Sometimes, I simply utter a compliment to encourage a person in an area where I sense a lack of confidence. You should see how a person's face lights up when he hears a timely compliment!

How can you help uplift other people? An uplifting gesture is priceless, especially to a demoralized person. There are numerous ways to encourage people, but the important thing is to be sincere. If you know a sick, mourning, or depressed person, send them a flower, an encouraging note, or gift. Let them know that you are also praying for them. The power of prayer is undeniable. A sincere prayer of faith can uplift people who are miles away from us.

"Sometimes our light goes out but is blown again into instant flame by an encounter with another human being."
~Albert Schweitzer

VISION

"Where there is no vision, the people perish."~Proverbs 29:18 (KJV)

Vision is the ability to perceive something not visible, a force of power or imagination. It is the art of seeing the invisible. In this respect, vision is not just seeing. Instead, it is the ability to see something that only you can picture. Others can't see or experience your vision because it is in your mind, exists in your imagination, and within yourself.

A vision is not a mere goal. It is something bigger, something that transcends a numerical target or human recognition. A vision compels a dreamer to pursue their dreams. It is bigger than our selfish ambition, and it is something that has the power to ignite our passion and willingness to sacrifice. Therefore, it is vital to have a vision of your life, in addition to dreams and goals. Our visions may be unique and different from others, making them ours to achieve.

William Wilberforce envisioned a nation free from the inhumanity of slavery. Steve Jobs envisioned a generation enjoying a digital lifestyle. Spiritually vision is a supernatural experience that conveys into reality. We must pursue God-given visions; it does not matter if people don't believe in it.

Mary, the mother of Jesus, had the vision to see her son grow up and fulfill what had been prophesied by the Angel Gabriel.

Finite and temporal goals do not have the power to sustain us through extreme trials. Nor do they t have the ability to satisfy our deepest longings for significance. But a vision has the power to do these. A vision can be abstract; it can be an idea or a concept. Vision is made real through creative work and human endeavor. A clear vision defines how successful you will be in conveying your vision to others. Vision is inspiration made reality. It is going beyond knowledge and reaching the artistic level. It is going beyond mastery and reaching improvisation and self-expression.

When I was in college, I had so many interests that I didn't know which one to pursue. So I asked God to give me a vision. The answer didn't come in a flash, but as I continued to ask God to reveal to me His will year after year after college, I slowly found myself putting pieces of the puzzle together until I finally saw God's vision for my life.

Do you have a vision that is bigger than your life and imagination? Don't settle for something ordinary and "possible" based upon your resources and ability. Instead, write down your vision for your life, family, and nation. Be specific. What does your vision look, feel, smell, sound, and taste? If you do not have one yet, pray for one and ask, what is your heart's greatest dream? That may be the key to your vision.

"Vision is the art of seeing what is invisible to others."
~Jonathan Swift

VISUALIZE

"Write down the revelation and make it plain on tablets so that a herald may run with it . . .Though it linger, wait for it; it will certainly come and will not delay." ~Habakkuk 2:2,3b (NIV)

To visualize is to imagine from a mental image or paint a picture of something in your mind. The primary benefit of visualization is it helps you to get more of what you want. When you vividly imagine achieving your goals, you trigger a whole series of subconscious processes that will help you reach your target. By training your brain to know what you want, you'll inevitably experience more real-world success.

Visualization is a powerful tool for accomplishing goals. If I ask you to sketch your bedroom, you'll visualize it first, right? We need to imagine before we execute. We tend to neglect this step. How can you work towards a vision which you cannot visualize with clarity? The more specific the detail, the easier it is to figure out what is needed to make it happen.

Have you heard of Nehemiah's story? He envisioned rebuilding the walls of Jerusalem. He didn't cast an incomplete vision, but he went through the details of the operations. Thus, when the king called him and asked him why he looked gloomy, he was instantly able to seize the king's favor and enumerate the resources needed for him to build those walls!

Don't let go of your vision! Visualize the details in your mind. That level of clarity may prove helpful when you suddenly meet favor and opportunity. Imagine bumping into a multi-millionaire and being asked, "What do you want other than money?" If your goals and vision aren't detailed, you can't give a specific answer.

Visualization fuels inspiration and magnetizes the resources needed for you to succeed. It stirs you up to 'keep on rolling.' However, there are instances when the dream is still too distant for us to devise a plan. Sometimes, we can only take preliminary steps and then hope to figure out what happens next after taking the first step.

When was the last time you visualized your dream? Make visualization a regular part of your schedule. Get a corkboard. Flip through magazines for photos that represent your dream; post them there, mark with today's date, and put a note like, "I'll be there soon!" Do you sketch? Draw what you see when your eyes are closed or when you are dreaming. Are you articulate with words? Describe in detail what you see in your mind. And every morning, look at that corkboard and keep that "picture" close to your heart.

"To dream by night is to escape your life. To dream by day is to make it happen." ~Stephen Richards

WIN

"Ask, and it will be given to you; seek and you will find; knock and the door will be opened to you." ~Matthew 7:7 (NIV)

To win means to achieve victory, success in an effort or venture. Winning is what distinguishes champions and winners from losers; it is the desire and passion to win. To win is to be successful in a contest or conflict. Ongoing motivation helps in building a winning attitude. How often do you bathe? Well, that's how often you need to expose yourself to motivation and self-improvement material. As Zig Ziglar said, "Motivation is not permanent, and neither is bathing." Understand the boost that you get is not permanent and that you need to keep absorbing motivation on an ongoing basis.

Sports enthusiasts know that winning teams have two things in common: skilled players determined to win. Usually, one or two players would stand out in their influence and determination to make the most of every game. These players exemplify not only skill but the ability to motivate and inspire their teammates. A three-time Olympic gold medalist who became a university basketball coach once said, "When you have that one person—that one individual who doesn't care about anything but winning—it's an amazingly powerful tool."

The winning mindset is more than just a desire to give one's best or flaunt one's skill, but the ability to reject anything that would say that you could not win this one.

Another quality of winners is their work ethic of sacrifice and commitment to be the best. To develop skill, one has to be consistent even in the mundane. Winning is not just one night in a baseball arena or a one-minute dance routine. Although mental strength is vital in those culminating moments in competition, the preparations behind the scenes are just as crucial.

If you desire to win in life, you must prepare by developing skills and experience. You must be ready to deliver during moments of repetitive victories and tremendous pressure. You must have a regular regimen that involves self-motivation. Your success will ultimately depend on your personal decisions rather than what others might think.

Stir up the competitive and warrior spirit in you. Set a goal this week to eat 50 percent fewer sweets and carbohydrates. Add a few more reps to your exercise routine. Read two more chapters in the latest book. Study a few more vocabulary words. Whatever you do, develop your winning strategy!

"It is not over until you win." ~ Les Brown

WISDOM

"The beginning of wisdom is this: Get wisdom. Though it cost all you have, get understanding." ~Proverbs 4:7 (NIV)

Wisdom is the soundness of an action or decision regarding the application of experience, knowledge, and good judgment. It means knowing what you know as well as what you don't know.

It has been said, "Knowledge will fill you with facts, but wisdom will show you how to use those facts properly." Even with the best education and most extensive professional experience, a man will lack wisdom without God. However, this does not in any way diminish the need for a good education. But wisdom is not achieved through a diploma or memorizing facts.

Most wise people will take the initiative to educate themselves in many subjects. While this requires a lot of patience, it is a tremendous asset when making decisions. However, you must first apply what you have learned.

A wise person will not squander his money or live beyond his means but will for discounts to save money on finances. He is not the type who impulsively buys things he doesn't need or can't afford but will save or invest their money.

But there is another kind of wisdom, one that is more costly. It means having insight into life's unsolvable problems by seeking wisdom from God. Proverbs 1:7 says, "The fear of the Lord is the beginning of wisdom." (NIV) When we fear God, we begin to discover the purpose of all the knowledge available to us. We grow in understanding and insight. We begin to see what we didn't see before. Our perspective changes, and we discover solutions that have always been there. Ask, pray and seek daily for wisdom. It will change how you make decisions and carry out your daily duties.

I have learned that wisdom often looks odd and different from our usual way of doing things. The best teacher on wisdom in the Bible is the book of Proverbs. Beginning with chapter one, read through the oracles and wisdom sayings of King Solomon. You don't have to be a Christian to gain something from the Bible, but I hope God will speak to your heart nevertheless.

"Wisdom is knowing the difference from right and wrong. It's the ability to recognize difference in yourself, a person, opportunity and an environment." ~Dr. Mike Murdock

XENIAL

"Do not forget to show hospitality to strangers, for by so doing some people have shown hospitality to angels without knowing it." ~Hebrews 13:2 (NIV)

Xenial is hospitable, cordial, open-minded, generous, especially to strangers and foreigners. Being kind and showing hospitality towards people brings blessings into your life. Unfortunately, many of us tend to fear strangers or simply do not care about them. But those who have this trait would consider people in need who cross their path as opportunities to extend their gracious service and hospitality.

Being hospitable towards someone creates an emotional bond. The body produces Oxytocin, the bonding hormone. It binds to the lining of your blood vessels and causes the dilation of the arteries. It results in a reduction of blood pressure. Oxytocin is a cardio-protective hormone. At the same time, kindness benefits the nervous system. The longest nerve in the human body is the vagus nerve that controls inflammation in the body. It plays a role in keeping your cardiovascular system healthy. People who are xenial have a more active vagus nerve. Therefore, xenial people must be cautious dealing with strangers. At the heart of this trait is empathy and kindness towards those who are in need. Xenial is not only showing kindness but also being brave when everybody is either afraid or unwilling.

And based on experience, helping people, I don't know that well, have opened doors to many good things. That's because strangers understand that you were under no obligation to help them. But, on the other hand, they may be more than willing to return your kindness in a way that you could not imagine.

When you do good things, good things happen to you. But more importantly, it brings out the good in people.

Are you a [xenial] context of word type of person? You can cultivate this trait in you. For example, do you pass the homeless on your way to work? Prepare a gift for them, such as an unused blanket, a restaurant gift card, or a bus pass. Gather some boldness and give them an early holiday present the next time you're doing daily errands.

"How far you go in life depends on your being tender with the young, compassionate with the aged, sympathetic with the striving, and tolerant of the weak and strong. Because someday in your life you will have been all of these." ~George Washington Carver

XEROPHYTIC

"But blessed is the one who trusts in the Lord, whose confidence is in him. They will be like a tree planted by the water that sends out its roots by the stream. It does not fear when heat comes; its leaves are always green. It has no worries in a year of drought and never fails to bear fruit." ~Jeremiah 17:7-8 (NIV)

Xerophytic means being able to adapt and withstand tough times; it is critical to pursue your dreams. When it feels your entire world is falling apart, this is the time you need to stand firm, strong, and stay optimistic.

Xerophytes are species of plants capable of surviving in a desert environment. A Xerophytic person emerges out from 'nothing' to 'everything' in life. Like those plants, the person can fight against all adverse conditions and move ahead to grow.

Xerophytes have three unique qualities: First is their ability to limit water loss through either waxy or fewer stomata (or openings). The second is their ability to store water through succulent stems, succulent leaves, or fleshy tubers. The third one is what most impresses me. They have deep root systems that dig way below the ground to reach sources of water!

Some of them also have the extreme ability to absorb surface water.

How do we apply this to our lives? First, when everything the world hurls at us seems to dehydrate us, we need to learn to preserve our sources of refreshment. Do you have a dream, a hope, or a promise? Keep it close to your heart!

Second, we need to store up encouragement, hope, inspiration, and faith. Do you have a journal where you keep fond memories and promises from God? You should! Store up truth and encouragement in your journal, in your heart when you memorize Scripture, and in your memory when you practice thankfulness. Write down or print out your three favorite Bible verses or quotes. Post them on your dresser, mirror, or the front page of your planner.

In the Bible, water represents the Word of God. So dig deep in the Word every day, and when adversity comes, your roots will be able to draw life from God's word. Dig your roots deep like a xerophyte, even before you reach the desert.

"It is not the strongest of the species that survives, nor the most intelligent that survives. It is the one that is the most adaptable to change." ~ Charles Darwin

YEARN

"You will seek me and find me when you seek me with all your heart." ~Jeremiah 29:13

To yearn is to have a strong desire and longing for something more profound than mere addiction or craving. Yearning, compared to desiring, connotes a need that is too difficult for words. In Psalm 84, David describes how his soul "yearns" for God and that his "heart and flesh cry out" for God. Yearning has an element of desperation that is no longer limited to his thoughts and feelings. This yearning is so powerful that it affects his flesh or body. At its core, yearning comes from the heart and the soul.

Yearning comes from God. He put it in us for him to satisfy. From all ranks of life, human hearts yearn for beauty, adventure, for recognition. There is a yearning to know, to comprehend, to experience, and to commune. God loves our yearnings. He wants to meet us in our place of hunger for more.

Yearnings give us the passion for learning and the motivation to grow. These desires pull us toward our dreams enabling us to make sacrifices. As long as you yearn for something, you can't congeal; there is a forward motion to yearning. When you are attracted to something, the attraction stirs your soul's yearning for connection to spirit, love, peace, joy, and possibility. And yet, many of us quickly complicate or negate this simple natural impulse for something different or better by creating excuses and stories.

However, the downside of yearning is disappointment. Some years my 2-year-old nephew became upset when I had to cut my trip short. I was devastated when he burst into tears. He was anticipating my longer stay but was sad by the change in plans. It is unfortunate, but setbacks are a part of life.

Although yearning can lead to disappointments, this does not mean that we should give up our dreams. On the contrary, if we cannot learn to deal with disappointment, we will never open ourselves to the possibility of becoming successful.

Our yearnings and passions are overwhelmed by the sheer volume of information thrown at us every day. If you want to rediscover your heart's true yearnings, try to reduce some time spent on news and entertainment and pray instead. What is your deepest yearning? Reflect, go deep within and tap into your true purpose. Could it be it is for a more spiritual life?

"To burn with desire and keep quiet about it is the greatest punishment we can bring on ourselves." ~Federico García Lorca

YIELD

"But the seed on good soil stands for those with a noble and good heart, who hear the word, retain it, and by persevering produce a crop." ~Luke 8:15 (NIV)

Yielding means being productive and having a return for an effort or investment. For a good yield, working smart is sometimes more important than working hard. Working smart means identifying which aspects of your investment will contribute to your increase with an application of wisdom, knowledge, and foresight. It helps us become more productive regardless of limited time and resources.

According to time investment philosophy, time is a limited resource and aligned with your definition of success. Therefore, the effort is required to gain maximum yield out of limited time. Considering that you have a limited time budget, you should understand that you can't do everything, regardless of your efficiency. The moment you embrace that truth, you instantly reduce your stress and feelings of inadequacy. As a result, you will be able to decide where you will not spend your valuable time, improving your yielding capacity.

You need to manage your resources and time wisely. For example, let's assume you have $500 to start an Origami business. If you spend it on paper and labor, you will be able to produce 1,000 Origamis to sell at $2.50 each! On the other hand, if you spend the money on paper and a solar-powered origami-folding machine, you will produce 2,000 Origamis to sell at $1 each. Which option will you take? It seems that option one will give higher earnings the first week, right? But you can also argue that buying a machine means you will not have to spend on labor the following week because the machine does not have an hourly wage. The point is, we need to work smart to get a better yield. We need to learn how to maximize our resources o lessen stressors in life.

Not all yields happen overnight. According to T.F. Hodge, "It takes time, patience, productivity and persistence to pop the oil; just keep digging." Likewise, worthy investments need time to show positive returns.

To have a good yield, you have to invest a combination of time, energy, and money. Are you spending too much money on school but reaping very little because you can't focus well on your studies? Invest quality time in studying, producing a better yield on tuition investment. The same thing applies to courting a girl, managing a house, and building an empire.

"Nothing is less productive than to make more efficient what should not be done at all." ~Peter Drucker

ZEAL

"Whatever your hand finds to do, do it with all your might, for in the realm of the dead, where you are going, there is neither working nor planning nor knowledge nor wisdom."
~Ecclesiastes 9:10 (NIV)

Zeal is having an enthusiastic devotion to a cause or goal and tireless diligence in its furtherance. It is a fervent or enthusiastic devotion, often extreme or fanatical in nature, as to a religious movement, political cause, ideal, or aspiration.

J.C. Ryle's preaching on "Christian Zeal" says that "Zeal in Christianity is a burning desire to please God, to do His will, and to advance His glory in the world in every possible way."

As long as you are alive, be zealous for a cause and be passionate for God. J.C. Ryle mentions that Christians are set apart by their zeal. If any people have the better ability to exemplify this trait, it should be Christians because of the enabling of the Holy Spirit and the love of God in their lives!

Zeal is a virtue that makes you bring about the glory of God with great enthusiasm and affection. Your zeal must be charitable and courageous, making you act with strength and gentleness.

Have you heard of Hudson Taylor, the first missionary to the interior of China? He was so set on preaching Jesus in mainland China he lived his life in preparation for the tough life he had to face. Before he left for China as a missionary, he got rid of his feathered bed and slept on hard boards to prepare him for his life as a missionary. By the age of nineteen, he taught himself to rely solely on God for his basic needs;

Can we be zealous for God, for justice, and the worthy causes life presents to us? On the one hand, it is frightening to be in a position to sacrifice great things for God. But, on the other, to live a life filled with zeal for a cause worth dying for seems to be the only way to live a full, exciting, and satisfying one.

Is there a need for more zeal in your life? Pray for your passion and for your purpose in life to be ignited. For example, are you working to eradicate poverty? Go through those facts and figures that once lit that flame in your heart. When I want my zeal for God to be re-ignited, I try to remember the passion that Jesus endured. I remember Jesus' zeal for my salvation. He is the author of the genuinely zealous and righteous life.

"A zealous person in Christianity is preeminently a person of one thing." ~J.C. Ryle

ZEST

"With joy you will draw water from the wells of salvation." ~Isaiah 12:3 (NIV)

Zest is enthusiasm and passion for pursuing a goal or objective. It is the liveliness or energy animating spirit. The opposite of zest is apathy, lethargy, dullness, or blandness. But, just like inspiration, zest cannot be forced out of us. I have met people who have that inspiring zest for life, and I have also encountered hopelessly lethargic people. Nevertheless, zest can change our perception of what life throws at us.

Zest is living life with a sense of excitement, anticipation, and energy. It's approaching life as an adventure, like motivation in challenging tasks. People who have zest exude excitement and energy while approaching tasks in life. Zestful people never give up; they simply enjoy things more than people who are not zestful. It's a positive trait that shows a person's approach towards life with anticipation, energy, and excitement.

I have a close friend who rejoices immensely at even the most trivial good news. I love to watch her become giddy when she receives the tiniest act of kindness. I sometimes feel ashamed at how I respond to good things that come my way. This friend has taught me to be more grateful. She is also an ambassador of excitement. She dresses up every day as if each day is extra special. She talks about how thankful she is for this and that. When something good happens to others, she rejoices with them and claims that the same will happen to her. People love to be around her, and they easily forgive her for her boisterous laughter. Her joy is heartfelt and contagious.

I love being around people who have a zest for life. I love people excited to do the work, whether it is a mundane task or a challenging one. We can live life with diligence for work and yet without a zest for the heartwarming blessings it gives.

To regain zest, we need to remember our created purpose. What has God called you to do? We all need to recognize that more extraordinary things await each one of us. The Bible says, "Hope deferred makes the heart sick." (Proverbs 13:12 NIV) When we lose hope in the future and lose the ability to pursue our passions, we lose our zest for life. But if we will give God our dulled heart, He will bring it back to life. His ultimate desire is for us to live lives full of zest for the grace He gives us every day.

Add zest to your life by declaring the reasons you are blessed. If you have not discovered your life's purpose, in time, your purpose will be revealed. Declare something like this every day upon waking up: "I am excited to fulfill my purpose for this day. I am blessed to possess the ability to bless others. I am eager to give my best in what I do!"

"If things don't come easy, there is no premium on effort. There should be joy in the chase, zest in the pursuit." ~Branch Rickey

ABOUT THE AUTHOR

Emelia's a Christian, kingdom-minded and passionate about spreading the goodness and greatness of God. She emigrated from her motherland country of Ghana –West Africa to the USA with nothing but dreams of a better life. She overcame many challenges, including near homelessness but stayed determined, focused, and worked hard to pursue her dreams.

Emelia is driven, authentic and down to earth. She's constantly reinventing herself and setting new goals. She's about purpose and living a fulfilled life. She's committed to using her life experiences to empower and inspire others to pursue their dreams and reach their full potential. By drawing from her personal and professional experiences, Emelia uses practical principles and strategies to mentor people to break through barriers that stop them from making their dreams a reality.

She's compassionate and has a big heart for giving and helping the poor and needy. She volunteers at food banks and shelter homes. She runs a non-profit organization called "Empower The Children – ETC" that supports orphans and less privileged children in Africa. ETC provides free food, clothing & toiletries to low-income communities. The foundation serves the youth through free education and resources to broaden their knowledge and perspective on life to become good productive citizens. The organization also donates books to schools and medical supplies to hospitals and clinics. One of her favorite quotes is ~ "I alone cannot change the world, but I can cast a stone across the waters to create many ripples," by Mother Teresa

Her mission is to inspire, transform lives and make a difference in diverse ways. Her hobbies are writing, reading, organizing, and enjoying the outdoors. She is a girly girl who enjoys shopping & make-up. She appreciates the simple and thoughtful things in life. Emelia is funny and doesn't take herself so seriously. She has sweet tooth and will choose dessert over a meal.

She's thankful and humbled by the opportunities God has blessed her. Her mission is to inspire, transform lives and make a difference in diverse ways.

Author's Contact Information:

Name: Emelia Adjei
Website: www.EmeliaAdjei.com
Email: info@EmeliaAdjei.com
Twitter—@ Emelia_Adjei
Facebook—@ Emelia Adjei—KPF

REFERENCES

Unless otherwise indicated, all definitions are from the Oxford Dictionaries. 2013, http://oxforddictionaries.com/us/.

i. See http://dictionary.reference.com/browse/etiquette

ii. See http://meditationdirectories.com

iii. Farlex (2013). Mindset. The Free Dictionary. Retrieved from http://www.thefreedictionary.com/mindset

iv. Negotiation (2013). Wikipedia. Retrieved from
v. http://en.wikipedia.org/wiki/Negotiation

vi. Farlex (2013). Opportunity. The Free Dictionary. Retrieved from http://www.thefreedictionary.com/opportunity

vii. Reinvent. Merriam-Webster Online. Retrieved from http://www. merriam-webster.com/dictionary/reinvent

viii. Oxford Dictionaries. http://www.yourdictionary.com/ visualize

ix. Xenial. Wiktionary. Retrieved from http://en.wiktionary.org/wiki/ xenial

x. Farlex (2013). Xerophytic, in Thesaurus. The Free Dictionary. Retrieved from http://www.thefreedictionary.com/xerophytic

Farlex (2013). Zeal, in Dictionary/thesaurus. The Free Dictionary. Retrieved from http://www.thefreedictionary.com/Zeals

xi. See http://dictionary.reference.com/browse/zest

xii. BibleGateway—http://www.biblegateway.com/versions/ New-International-Version-NIV-Bible/

Google—www.google.com

www.ingramcontent.com/pod-product-compliance
Lightning Source LLC
Chambersburg PA
CBHW071458070526
44578CB00001B/380